JAPANESE RESIDENCE

Edited by Takahiro Ohashi

images
Publishing

Contents

Foreword

Historical Japanese Architectural Styles

Japan historically has a legacy of upper-class housing that still influences Japanese architecture today. These buildings incorporated a myriad of elements, such as politics, culture, and daily life, and fused them into a unique construction method. There are many examples of modern Japanese houses that inherit these traditions.

Historical Japanese architecture can be divided into three major categories: *shinden-zukuri*, *shoin-zukuri*, and *sukiya-zukuri*. (The word '*zukuri*' means 'style.')

Shinden-zukuri, derived from a Japanese word for a mansion used primarily for sleeping, was established during the Heian period (794-1185). It was the style of the upper class at the time. *Shinden-zukuri* most emphasizes elegance and harmony with nature.

Heian culture deeply respected nature and the four seasons, as evidenced by the prominence of the *Waka*, a 31-syllable poetic form that often used nature as a theme. As a result, trees and artificial ponds could commonly be found among mansions from this time period.

Architecturally, the mansion is generally surrounded by a *nure-en* (an open corridor), while the interior just has pillars and almost no walls. The interior can be accessed from many angles, as doors are placed on all sides of the house, allowing free flow of fresh air during the daytime.

As *shinden-zukuri* developed over time, the style eventually into a whole new style: *shoin-zukuri*.

Starting in the Muromachi period (1336-1573) and lasting until the early Edo period, *shoin-zukuri* emphasized creating a sort of aristocratic study. In fact, *shoin* in Japanese means 'study.' Over time, mansions went beyond just an everyday residence and were transformed into ceremonial spaces, which likely can be attributed to the rise of samurai, a social class particularly concerned with ritual. The main room, or *shoin*, consists of a writing desk, a window for light, some book shelves, and tatami mats. While in *shinden-zukuri*, the interior was an open space, in *shoin-zukuri*, various types of partitions were used, such as *fusuma* (a sliding panel with painted scenes) and *shoji* (a room divider made of translucent paper covering a wood frame).

Sukiya-zukuri emerged during the Azuchi Momoyama period (1573-1603). This style encouraged a more personalized look. While the period still paid close attention to projecting status, many elites disliked elaborate decorations and opted for designs that were simple yet sophisticated. In addition, *sukiya-zukuri* used materials and techniques that at the time were rather unfamiliar. For example, rather using conventional white plaster walls, the walls often were given a soil finish. Also, the eaves are long, bringing deep silence to the interior space. However, as time went on, especially after the Edo period, *sukiya-zukuri* began using ever more elaborate materials and construction methods. At present, *sukiya-zukuri* has become particularly expensive, becoming synonymous with high-class architecture that requires advanced technology. *Sukiya-zukuri* can be commonly seen in high-end restaurants in Japan today.

Japanese Architecture in the Modern Era

In the Meiji era (1868-1912), there was no official regulation on architecture. More and more of western techniques were being incorporated into Japanese architecture, as a common belief at the time was modernization meant westernization. This incorporation of western techniques leads to many advancements in construction. Yet, the overall number of western houses was small, limited to upper-class individuals. Most people still carried out their day-to-day life in traditional Japanese housing.

Starting in the Taisho era (1912-1926), the urban middle-class started desiring a western-style life, and more and more houses began to appear that combine western and Japanese styles of architecture. Nonetheless, some features remained unchanged, such as the presence of tatami mats.

World War Two left a significant amount of Japanese housing devastated. Many low-quality barracks were put together to address the housing shortage. However, even after Japan entered high economic growth, the country still struggled with ever increasing demand for housing. This led to the popularization of cheap housing and the use of inexpensive materials, such as plywood.

After the liberalization of wood imports in 1960, cheap imported wood flooded the market, reducing construction costs of new buildings. Beginning in the 1970s, prefabricated houses have become popular, resulting in the mass production of housing. In recent years, Japanese houses have drifted far away from traditional construction, opting to use steel and concrete for materials and prefabrication for construction techniques.

Present and Future of Japanese Architecture

In the 1980s, it was most common for three generations of a family to live together in a single household. However, by 2015, the most common households in Japan have become couples and single adults.

With changes both to demographics and lifestyles as well as the development of technology, Japanese society requires the housing industry to adapt.

In the era where individuality is given special importance, the design of Japanese houses has also undergone great transformation. The house was a family's inherited things until 20 years ago. Now, it has become what one generation holds. Children grow up and leave their parents to find jobs. Many housing architects have come to address Japan's changing architectural landscape. Even though Japan has strict housing regulations, due to its frequent earthquakes, these architects all manage to find their own style, and breakdown of the traditional family dynamics has opened up new design spaces for them to explore.

As you will see in this book, the building area of many Japanese homes is small. Most are less than 1076 square feet (100 square meters) and some are even less than half the size, like the project Link mentioned in the book. Land is expensive in Japan, which has necessarily resulted in small living spaces. Because of the limited space, many Japanese have embraced minimalism in their homes, seeking only what is absolutely essential.

Given the aging population and declining birthrate, vacant houses are increasing, which is leading to new housing challenges. Renovation will be important to adapt them for the next generation. In addition, new technologies offer new benefits and problems as well. On one hand, retrofitting vacant buildings with new technology will be a costly and time-consuming endeavor. On the other hand, techniques like three-dimensional modeling can dramatically improve the efficiency of the design process. The projects listed in this book give a number of examples of how technology may change Japanese housing.

We are now living in the era of smartphones and tablets, a time where the internet is just in the palm of your hand. Children who have been using the internet practically since they were born are going to see the world with a very different set of eyes. Japanese architecture needs to reform itself to adapt to these on-coming changes. The architects presented in this represent the beginnings of that reformation.

Takahiro Ohashi
*studio LOOP

A Large Roof in the Forest

Design
Kazunori Tenkyu

Location
Kagawa

Completion
2014

Area
1392.5 square feet (129.37 square meters)

Photography
Kazunori Nomura

The site is located on the foot of a small mountain in Takamatsu. The southern side of the site is covered with trees, and the northwest side is open to the city. One can see for tens of kilometers when looking around from the site, connecting the site with the sky and the city. After revising the plan repeatedly, the composition ultimately made use of the material's characteristics.

Three pillars stand closely together in the living room representing the family members. They not only support the large roof but also exist in harmony with trees on the southern side. In addition, the architecture mirrors the topography, resulting in the building volume being toned down as a whole.

Second-floor plan

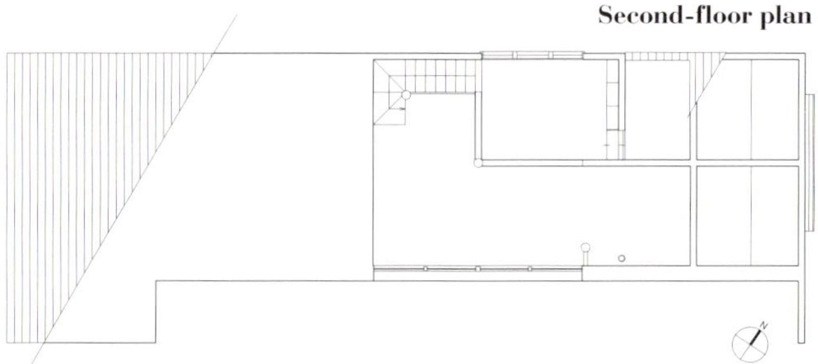

First-floor plan

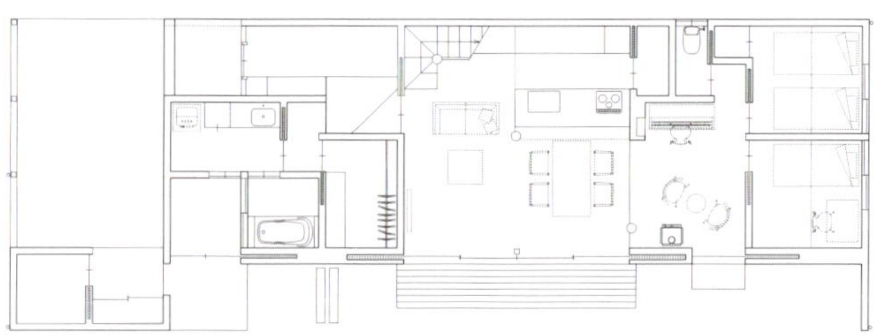

Alley House

Design
Takanobu Kishimoto

Location
Tokushima

Completion
2016

Area
981 square feet (91.14 square meters)

Photography
Eiji Tomita

The project, built for a husband, wife, and their daughter, sits on two flagstaff lots lying on both north and south-facing plots. The north-side lot will be used freely by the clients' daughter in the future. The family house is located south of the sites. The connection between north and south will be an important element in constructing their daughter's house on the north side in the future.

The narrow alley, one of the characteristics of flagstaff lots, was unaltered, meaning there is a narrow street connecting the north and south areas. Three factors of the clients' lives were taken into design consideration. The first was an area with water. The second was a space for the husband's hobbies. The third was a space for the mother and daughter. A space for family gatherings is located on the lane space of the house. The space can be accessed by passing through the narrow alley. The family area also allows them to access their respective spaces from there. In the future, the alley-shaped family space will connect these houses located on the north and south sides of the site.

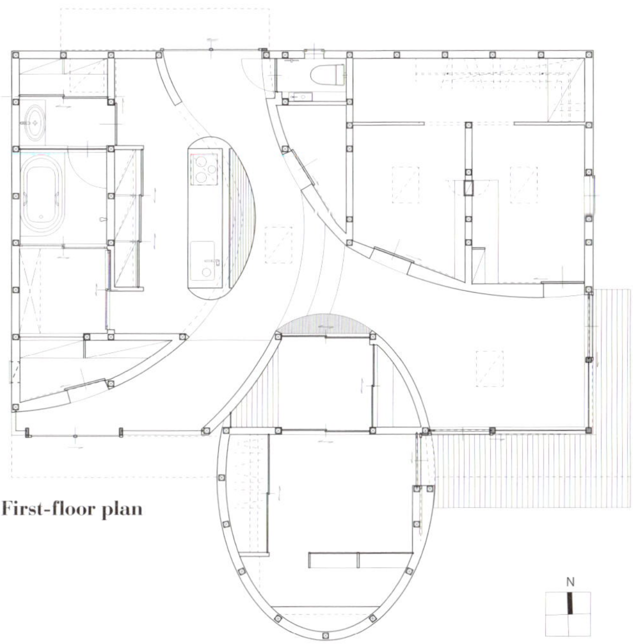

First-floor plan

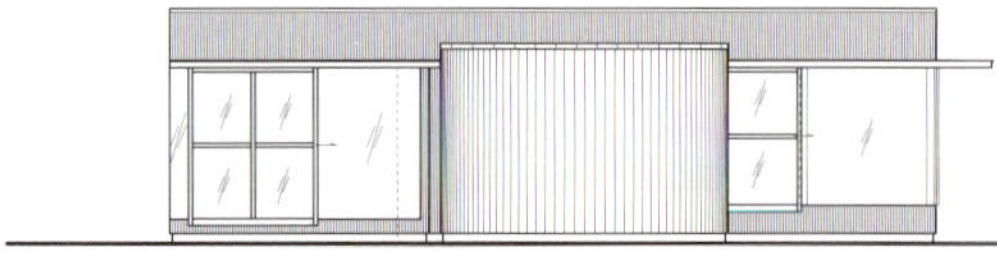

East elevation

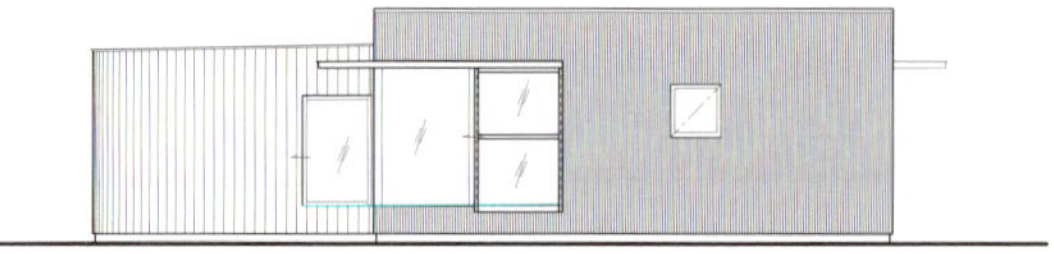

South elevation

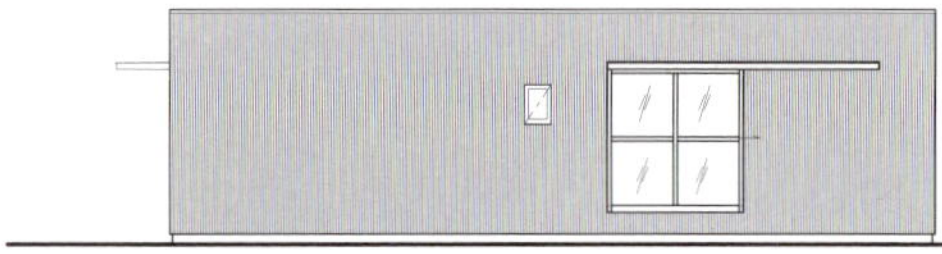

North elevation

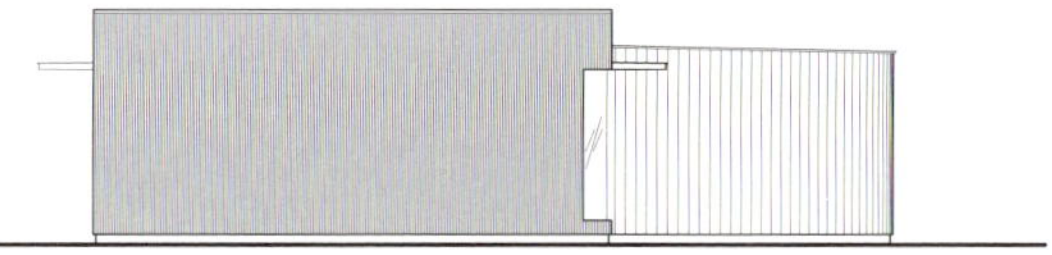

West elevation

Apartment House

Design
Kazuyasu Kochi
(Kochi Architect's Studio)

Location
Chiba

Completion
2014

Area
1069.6 square feet (99.37 square meters)

Photography
Daichi Ano, Kazuyasu Kochi

This is a renovation project of single-family house, originally used as a typical two-story apartment-house with eight small rental units. More than half of the units of this old wooden apartment were empty, therefore the owner wanted to demolish it and then build a new single-family house. However, the designer proposed to renovate this existing building into a single-family house instead of demolishing it. With the given budget, the designer thought the new building would only have half the area of the existing building.

The act of dividing coexists with the act of uniting here. The result is a dynamic and complex internal space, which provides the experience of all the spaces united without losing the ability to retreat to a personal space. In this project, the designer's ambition was to create a richness of diverse sceneries within this small architecture.

First-floor plan

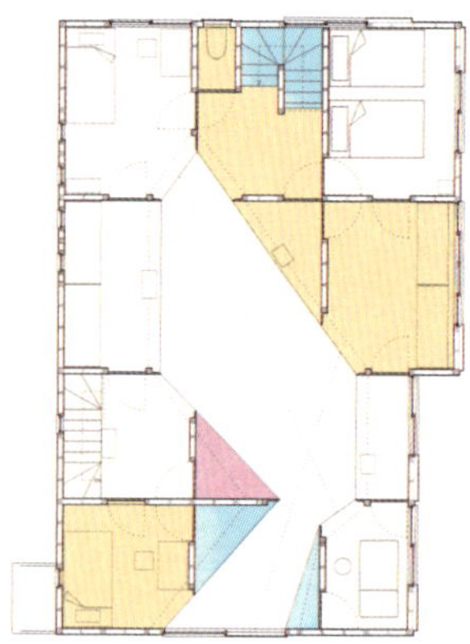

Second-floor plan

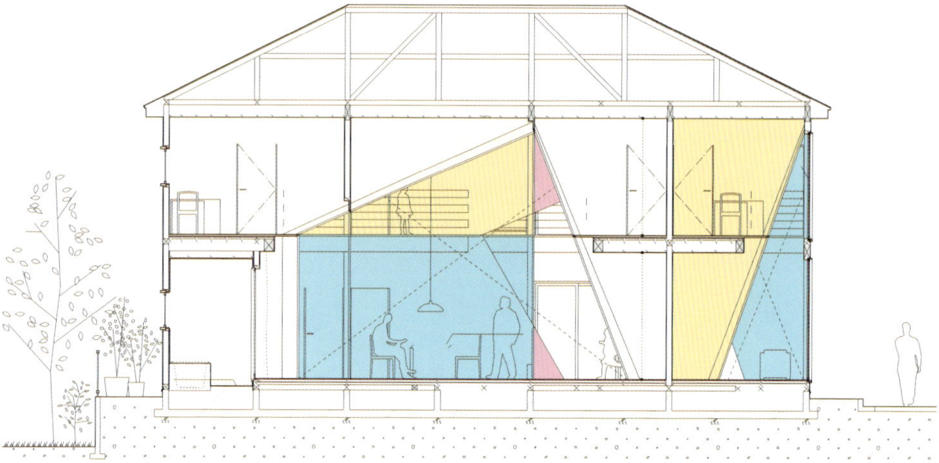

Section

Binocular House

Design
Masao Yahagi

Location
Ube, Yamaguchi

Completion
2015

Area
1810.3 square feet (168.18 square meters)

Photography
Kouichi Torimura

This house was designed for a couple and a child who wanted to live in a rich natural environment. Fortunately, they were able to build their home facing Lake Tokiwa. Initially, the land was a grove of scattered trees, and if the trees near the lake were cut down, the embankment of the lake would likely collapse. So, the designer decided to minimize cutting existing trees and designed the house to look like a pair of binoculars looking out towards the lake from the forest.

On the second floor, the master bedroom and the living room are located in different wings respectively. Each wing has been arranged at a different angle so the view of the lake is slightly shifted. On the first floor, the owner's hobby room and bathroom were placed in opposite wings. The empty area is a location for the client's wife to do gardening and grow vegetables. In between the two wings, the designer created a guest room on the first floor and a balcony on the second floor, as well as a courtyard in the center.

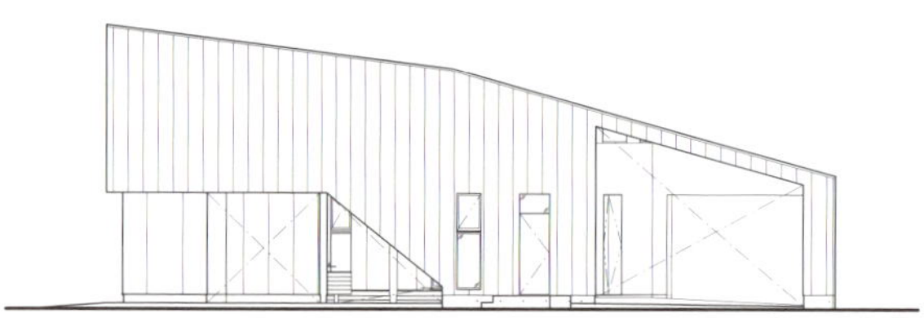

Elevation 1

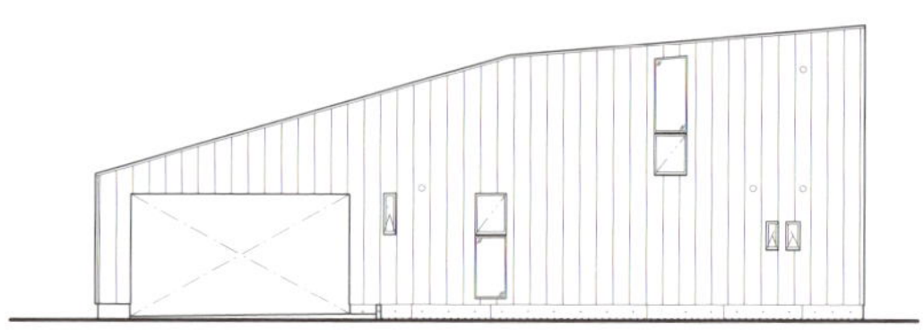

Elevation 2

Elevation 3

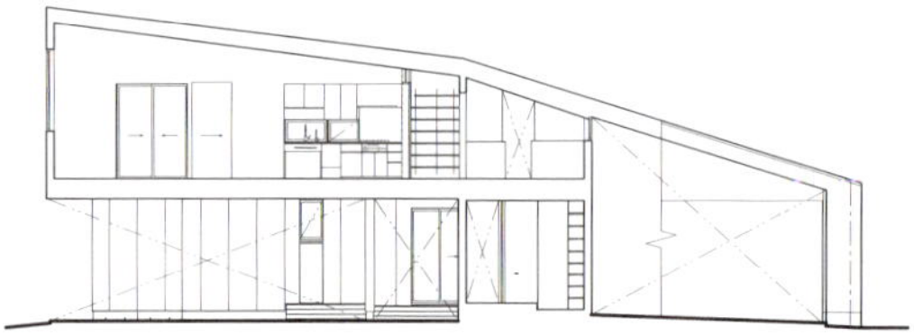

Section 1

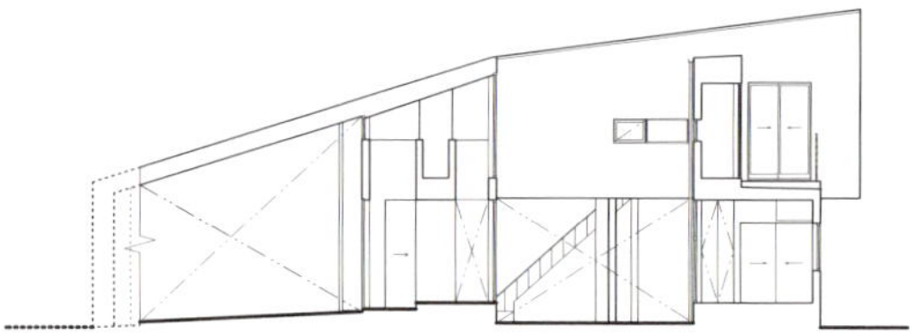

Section 2

Box Ouchi-06

Design
Jun Ishikawa, Naoko Ishikawa

Location
Fukushima

Completion
2014

Area
1151.7 square feet (107 square meters)

Photography
Hiroshi Ueda

The designer placed the master bedroom, a storage room, an auxiliary room on the first floor and designed a living room for the second floor. The visual is like a white box riding on a white diagonal wall. The oblique wall is in front of the bathroom and is made so that the interior cannot be seen from the outside.

Upon entering, there is a transitional space on the right, and the floor finish of the room is tatami mat. The space between this transitional room window and the oblique wall contains a small garden. Going left from the entrance, there is a master bedroom and a light garden. There are two children's rooms on the second floor. In the living room, there is a long window, which makes it difficult for the room to be seen from outside. From this living room, after climbing up a set of stairs, there is a large glass window, outside of which is a rooftop balcony surrounded by walls to muffle the sound of the railroad and to give some privacy.

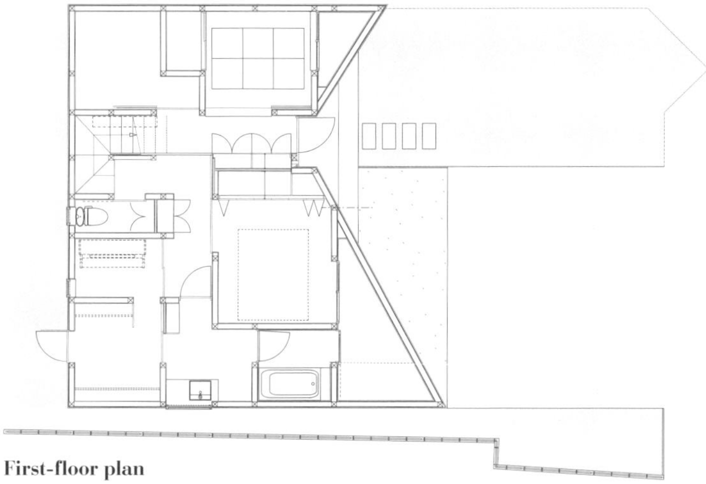
First-floor plan

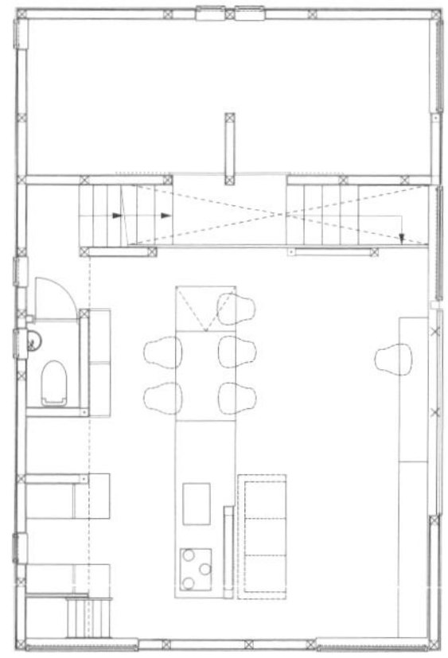
Second-floor plan

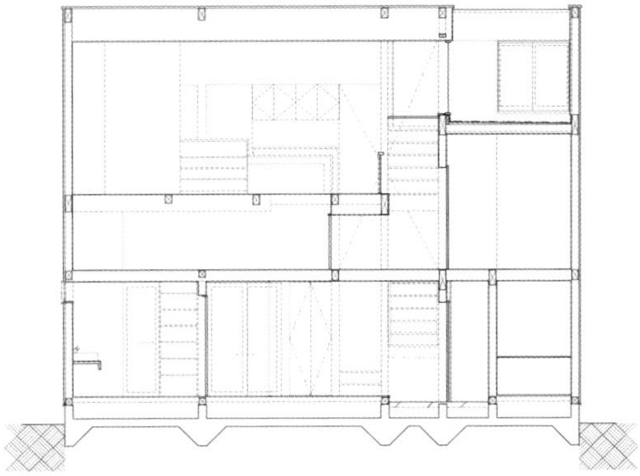

Section

Box Ouchi-08

Design
Jun Ishikawa, Kiyo Turu

Location
Tokyo

Completion
2015

Area
925.7 square feet (86 square meters)

Photography
Jun Ishikawa

This house was built with a *hako*-type design and a rooftop balcony. The design started from the owner's desire, 'I want to make the living room as large as possible.' In order to fulfill the above, the designer concentrated all the private rooms and bathrooms on the first floor and designed the second floor as one large space.

Entering the house, there is a stairway going up to the living room on the second floor. On the first floor, there is a master bedroom, children's room, and a spare room.

Above the low ceiling is a roof balcony and, in the living room, there is a stairway connected to the balcony. As you climb the stairs, there is a transparent floor along the east-facing window of the balcony, allowing light to scatter all over the living room floor.

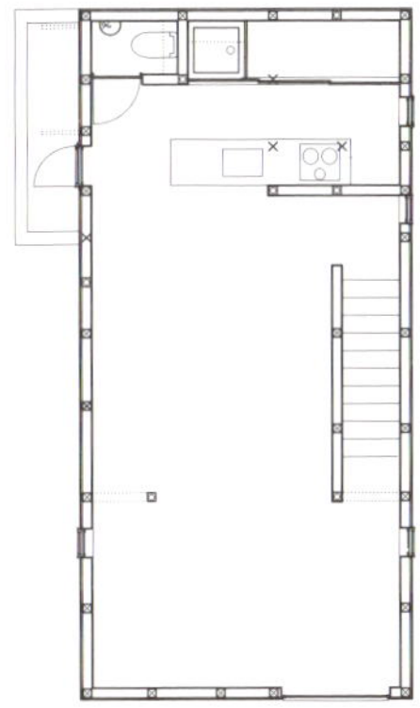

Second-floor plan

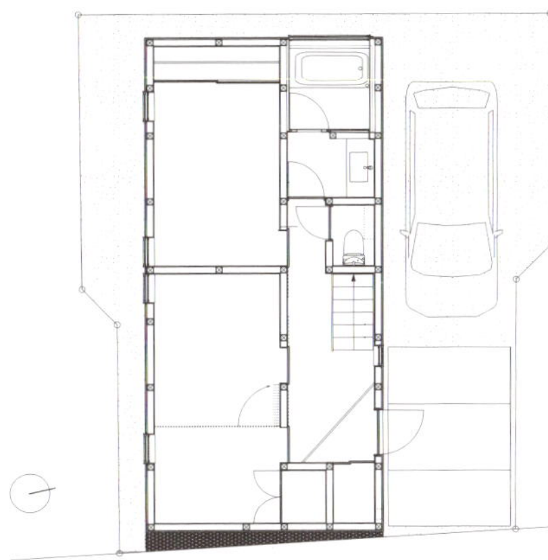

First-floor plan

Box Ouchi-10

Design
Jun Ishikawa

Location
Tokyo

Completion
2015

Area
1108.7 square feet (103 square meters)

Photography
Nobutaka Sawazaki

This three-story house was completed in Tokyo with a jacquard design. The plan was a three-story wooden building. Because the designers had to address strict height regulations in the construction, the FL on the first floor was placed lower than the GL and the height of the third floor was raised. Storage and bathrooms are on the first floor. The living room, dining room, and kitchen are on the second floor. The bedroom and children's room are on the third floor. The designers also placed space on the rooftop. The owner wanted a big window in the living room. Therefore, the team proposed a plan with a large opening on the south side. Fortunately, since the neighbor's exterior wall was a wall without windows, the designer was able to design a large window without concern for privacy. The window is made of custom-made steel, and by adopting heat-resistant tempered glass, the windows have clear visibility without resorting to fire-retardant glass. According to the regulations of Japan, the size of one window is limited to 32.3 square feet (3 square meters) in an urban area. Therefore, the designers placed together four windows of 32.3 square feet (3 square meters) to construct one large window. This large window has become a huge feature of this house and created an open living room looking up to the sky.

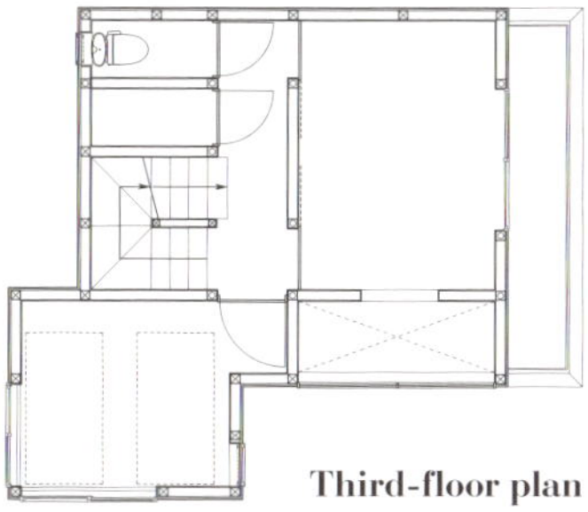

Third-floor plan

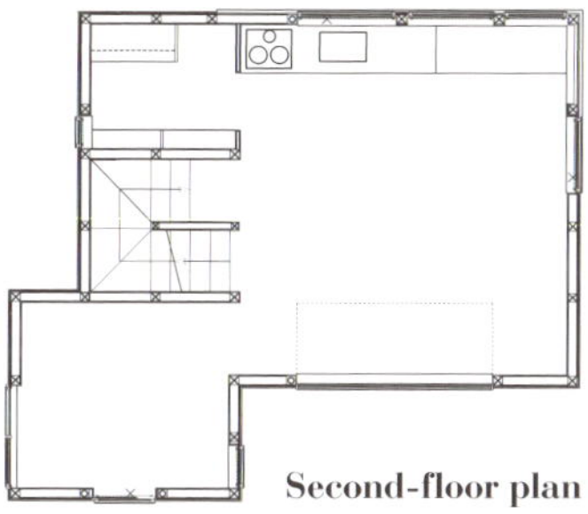

Second-floor plan

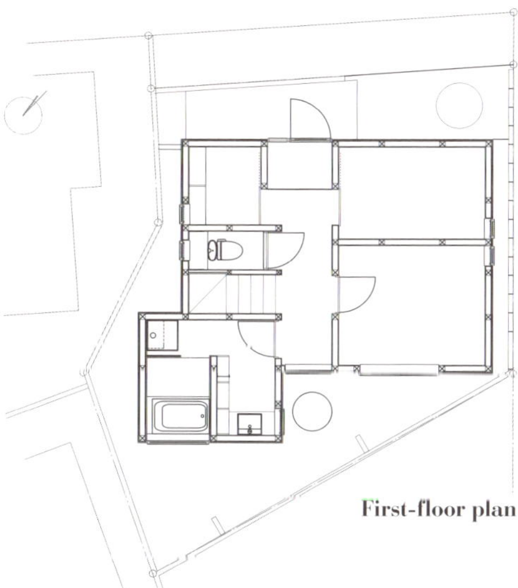

First-floor plan

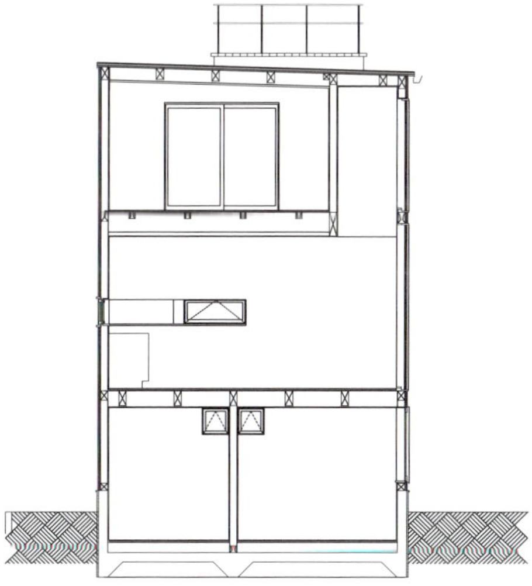

Section 1

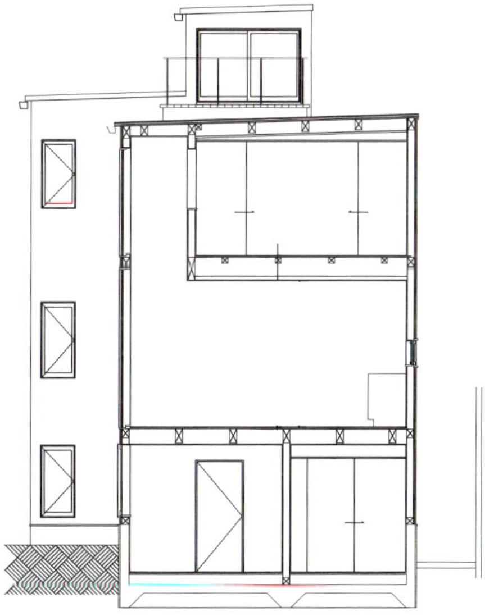

Section 2

Cardigan Cardigan!!

Design
Takeru Shoji

Location
Niigata

Completion
2015

Area
1028.8 square feet (95.58 square meters)

Photography
Isamu Murai

The open space in the front of the site is a parking space. However, the large roof is aimed at being an enclosure of the townscape with rich dynamics between the house and the town, as if inside and outside were inseparably connected to each other. Thus, the ordinary open space could create a significant communal atmosphere under a common roof.

The plan was simple. Residents were to mostly stay in the living room area on the first floor, and rest in their private rooms on the second floor. The design for the rooms placed a moderate distance among the family, often uniformly fixed, by creating a variety of places to attract people. The architects made good use of natural lighting with a large wooden slat for letting in warm sunlight during the winter and lattice flooring for vertical ventilation. With air flow from the ground floor to the roof as its only means of air-conditioning, Cardigan Cardigan!! is geared towards being a compact and efficient house covered with a large roof.

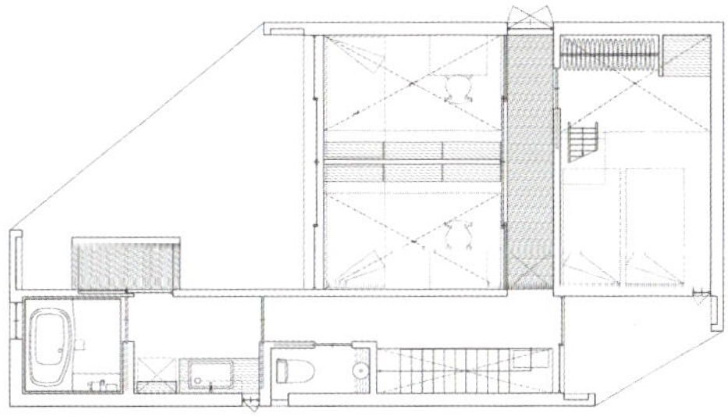

Second-floor plan

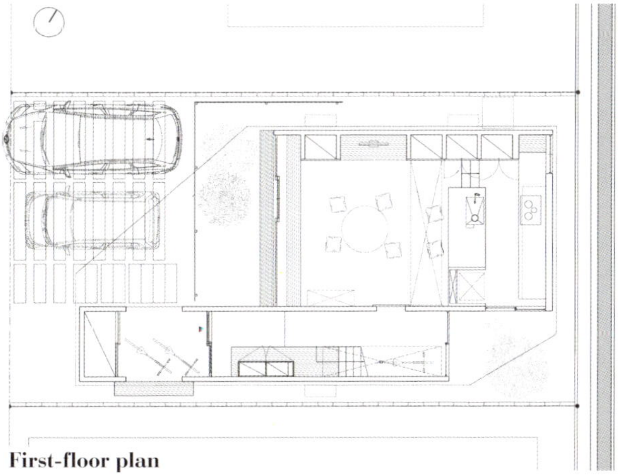

First-floor plan

Complex

Design
FORM / Kouichi Kimura Architects

Location
Shiga

Completion
2015

Area
5371.9 square feet (499.07 square meters)

Photography
Yoshihiro Asada

This project was an complex building, consisting of four floors including a garage on the first floor, an office on the second floor, and a guest house on the third and fourth floors.

The solid walls of the façade were finished with rough steel plates, which enhance the massiveness of the building. Meanwhile, the elaborately designed sections of the openings create a light appearance.

What characterizes the inner space of this building is the guest house designed on the third and fourth floors. The space of the two-tiered living room and the dining room/kitchen is flooded with light. The hallway that is laid out in the remaining space produces variation in the cross section of the ceiling and visual clearance. The natural light brings about a tender yet crisp atmosphere.

The impressive design, by making the best use of shade and shadow both in the external and internal spaces of the building, has become a local landmark characterizing the corporate image.

Section

Second-floor plan

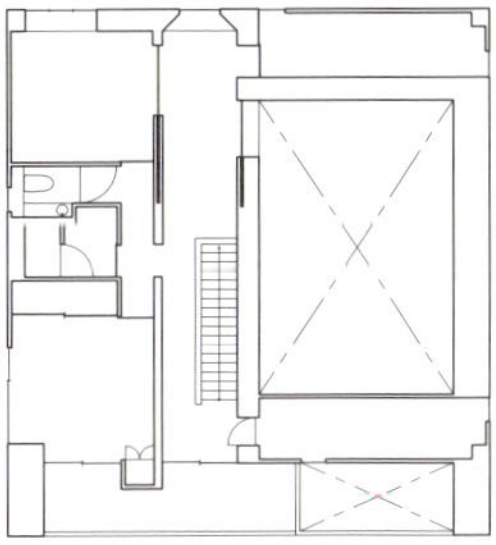

Fourth-floor plan

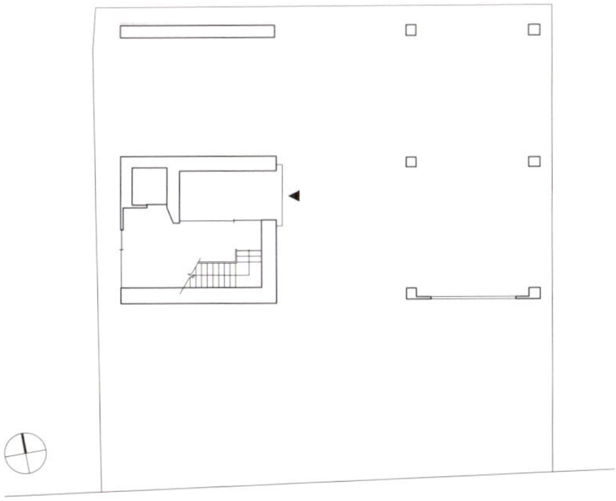

First-floor plan

Third-floor plan

Courtyard in Kudamatsu

Design
Takanobu Kishimoto

Location
Kudamatsu

Completion
2014

Area
775.4 square feet (72.04 square meters)

Photography
Eiji Tomita

The site is along a prefectural road. The ancestral home has been built at a point distant from the road. The client's main hope is that they can walk around their family home and their children can run around inside and outside the house. Their family home has a tiled roof and wooden front door. It is better that their family home is seen from the prefectural road, so their house was built near that road. As a result, the house was built like a gate and fence. The house sports a big roof, which pays homage to their ancestral home.

The house was made with a big opening toward the ancestral home. Thus, that has made them conscious about living within the ancestral home. In addition, their children can come and go between their ancestral home to the house and will not cross the prefectural road. The layout of the house is similar to the outside. This house was built with a number of safety considerations so that their children can run around without danger.

First-floor plan

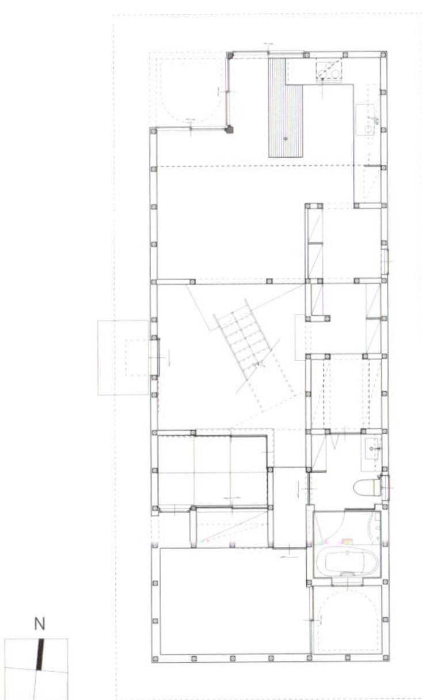

Second-floor plan

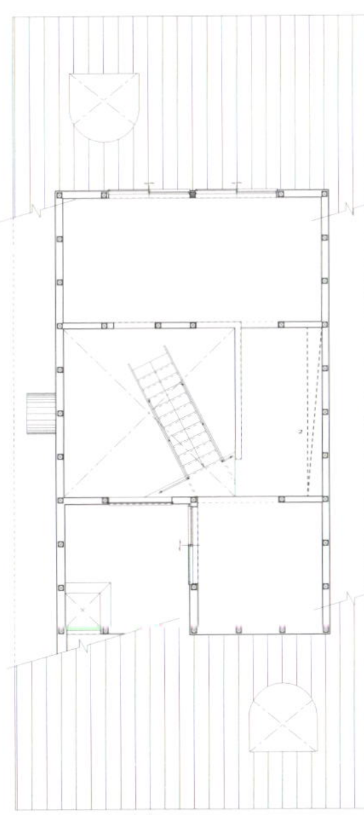

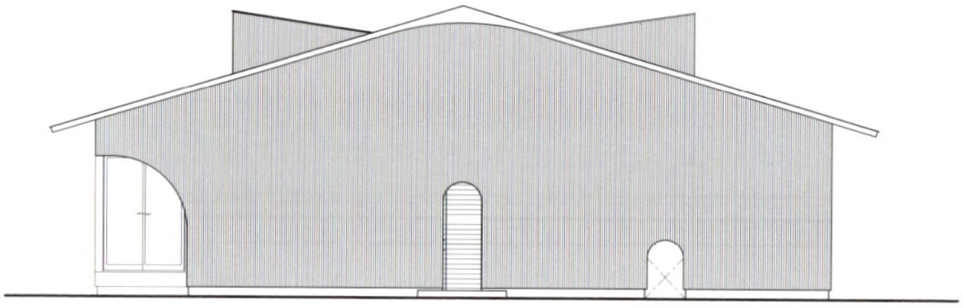

West elevation

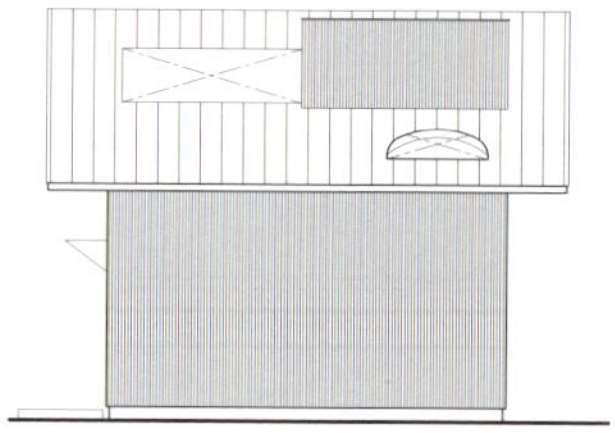

South elevation

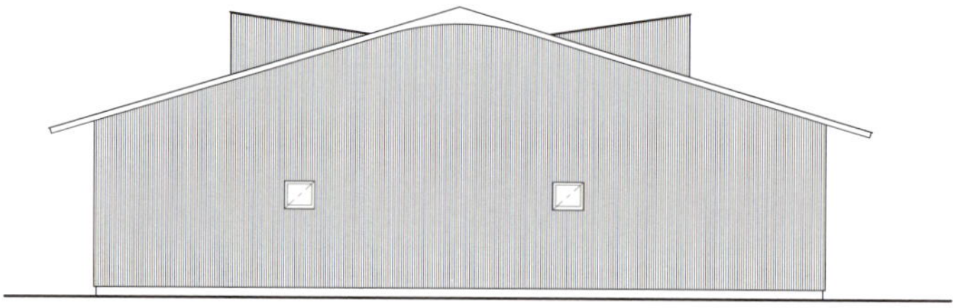

East elevation

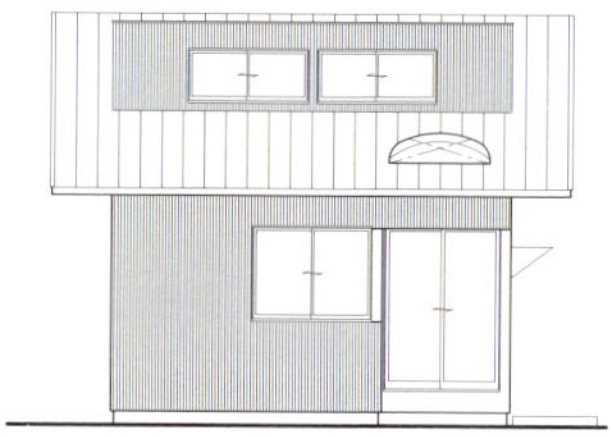

North elevation

Curved Roof House

Design
Hiromu Nakanishi Architects

Location
Kyoto

Completion
2015

Area
1544.6 square feet (143.5 square meters)

Photography
Kai Nakamura

The curved roof creates a link with both the neighboring buildings and the existing *machiya* structure as well as the interior with the exterior. To accomplish this design the designer referred to traditional Japanese garden designs, such as Murin-an and Entsuji Temple. The *machiya* is built in a traditional style, while the extension is in a modern style.

The exterior and interior finishes look traditional and natural, but the facilities and appliances are modern and sophisticated. The several air conditioners and the floor heating systems are completely hidden behind the traditional appearance.

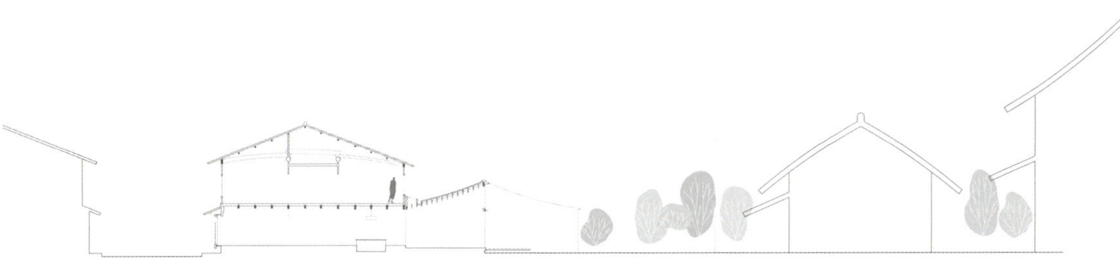

Section

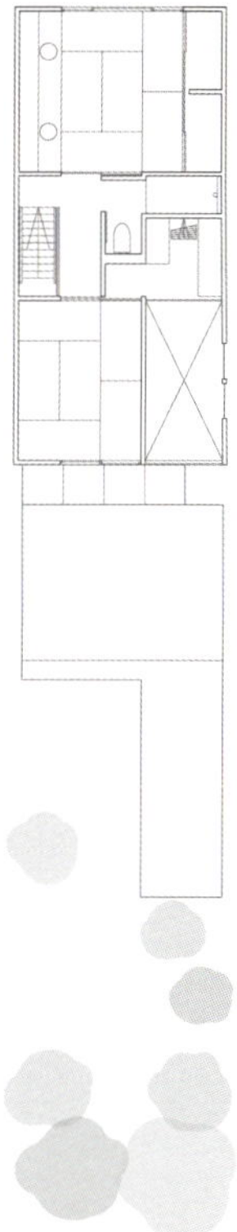

Second-floor plan

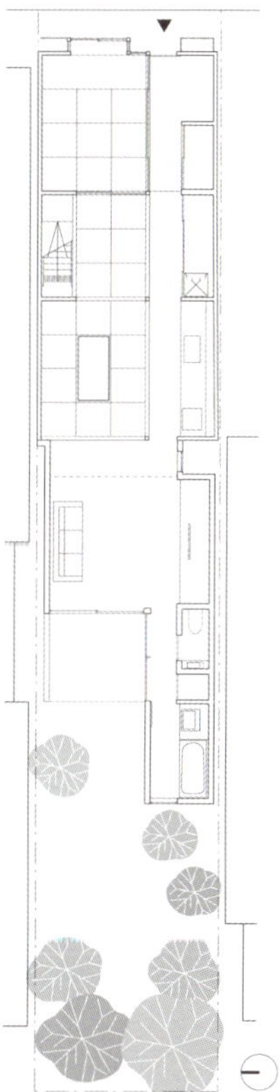

First-floor plan

Daiko

Design
Keitaro Muto

Location
Nagoya

Completion
2017

Area
1713.6 square feet (159.2 square meters)

Photography
Teruaki Yoshiike

The project is a three-story residence near central Nagoya. The truss being used as a side wall for the terrace has two effects. First, this cuts off the view of the neighbors and the front road, and another effect is framing the cityscape and sky. The interior has been divided into quarters to support the spacial needs. Huge openings have been made along the walls to give the rooms a stronger connection with each other. Elements such as stairs and wall openings have been placed to increase the sense of unity between the exterior and interior.

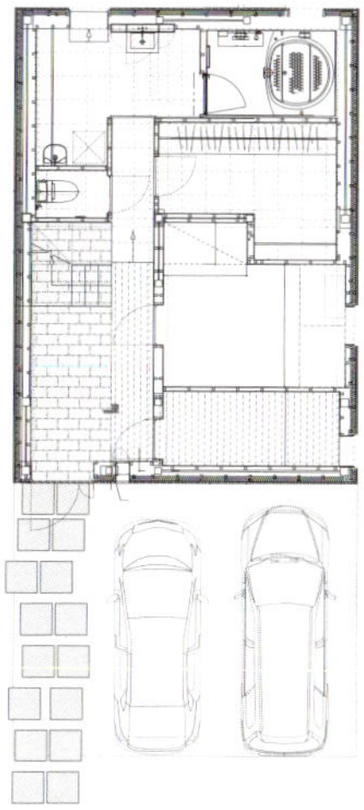

First-floor plan

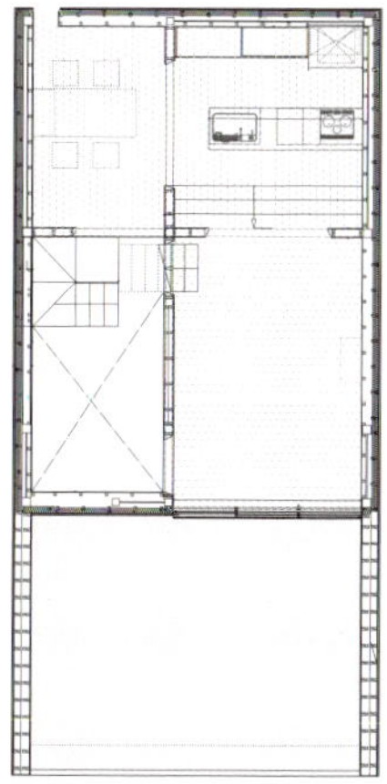

Second-floor plan

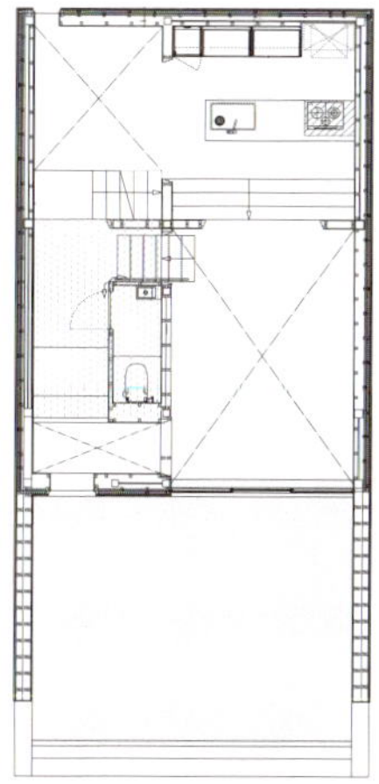

Mezzanine-floor plan

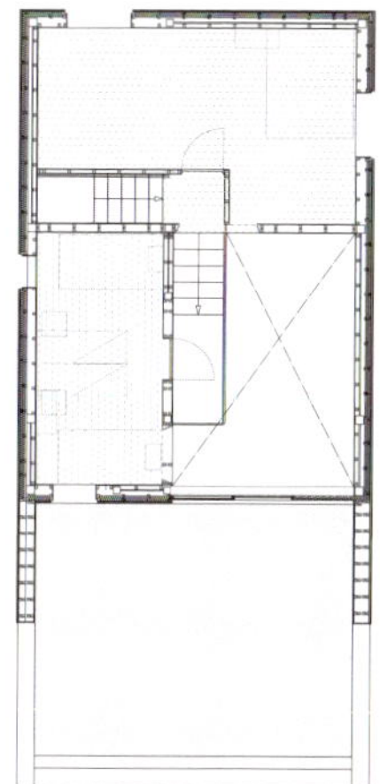

Third-floor plan

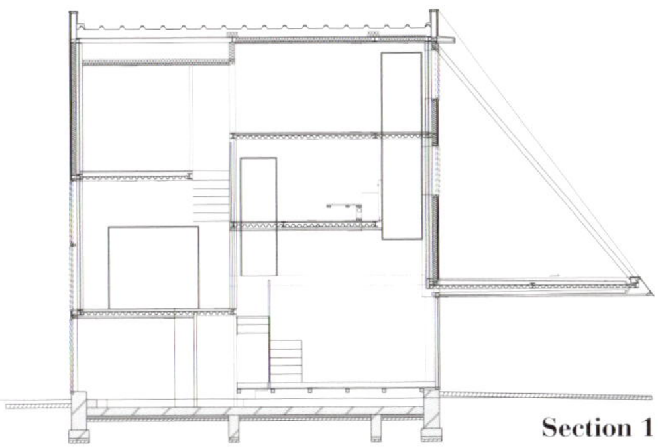

Section 1

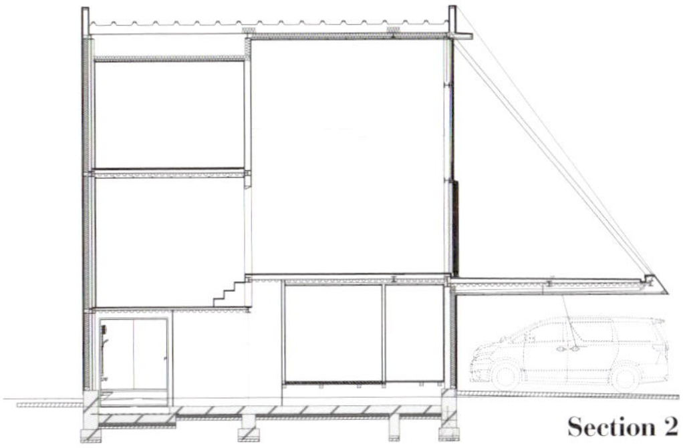

Section 2

Elephant House

Design
Hiromu Nakanishi Architects

Location
Kyoto

Completion
2014

Area
1023.2 square feet (95.06 square meters)

Photography
Kai Nakamura

The site of the house is situated beside Odoi, which was a river bank in the 16th century. Having previously been a riverbed, the landform of the site is sunken. The inner court is central to the structure of the house, as it introduces sunlight, ventilation, and greenery to all corners of the house. Besides, this house can function as either a single room or several rooms depending on conditions. The bathroom and sun room are usually opened toward the court for ventilation.

In the summer, the client can use the windows to emit heat, while in winter, the client can use the floor heating systems.

This architecture is built of wood. The structure is simply composed of an outer wall, an inner wall, and a roof. The designer created the space based on activities, atmosphere, and furniture here, rather than with a structural frame. The aim is to create diverse and unique spaces within a simple architecture.

First-floor plan

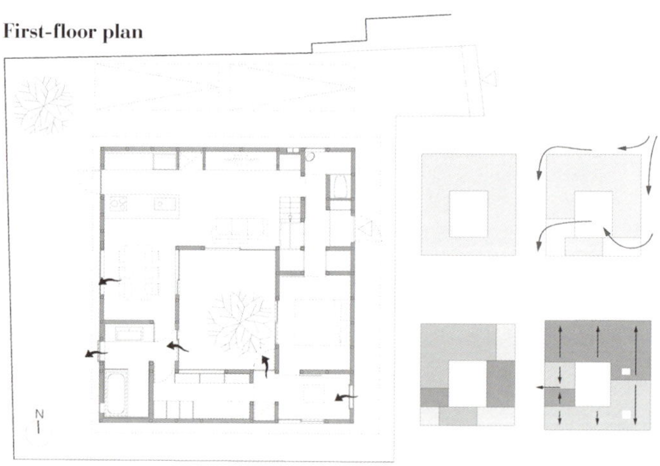

Second-floor plan

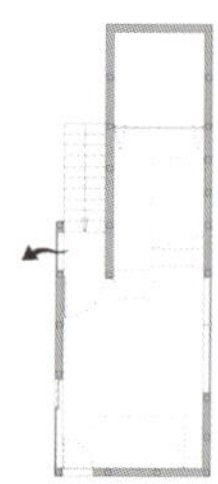

Axonometric

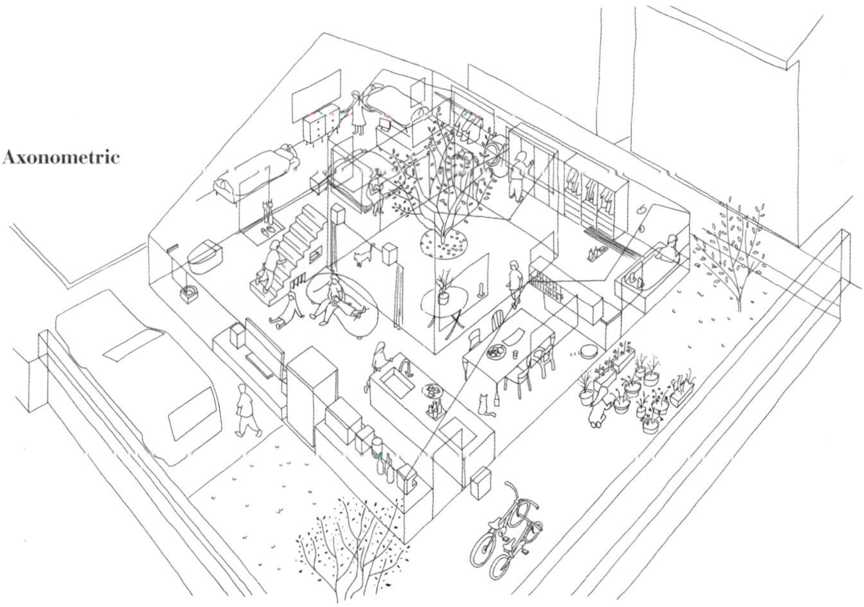

F Residence

Design
Shinichi Ogawa & Associates

Location
Gifu

Completion
2017

Area
2290.6 square feet (212.8 square meters)

Photography
Shinichi Ogawa & Associates, Toshiyuki Yano

The site is surrounded by vast rice fields on all sides. The plan suspends the building in the rice fields by raising the entire building from ground line. When first arriving at the house, you see a long bridge to the entrance floating in the paddy field. An office, living area, dining area, and kitchen are located on the south side. The north side consists of a master bedroom and a children's bedroom. A terrace extends the space, converging the inside with the outside, as if the interior were a part of nature. The core of the house consists of a bathroom and storage space, alongside of which is the courtyard, adding to the sense of openness. This building is surrounded by vast nature. In the spring, the residence 'floats' in the middle of the paddies; in the summer, the house 'floats' on blue-green rice shoots; in the fall, the rice stalks take on a golden color; and in the winter, the house 'floats' on a field of snow.

Plan

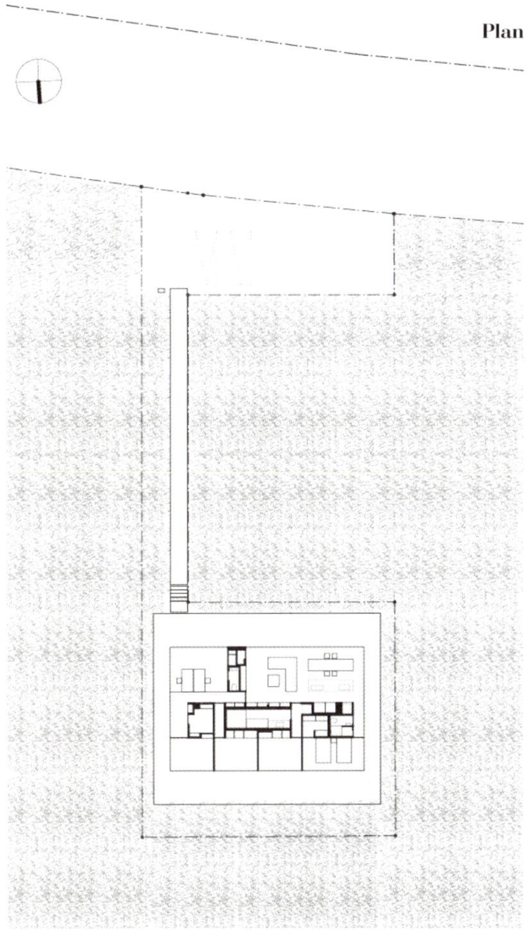

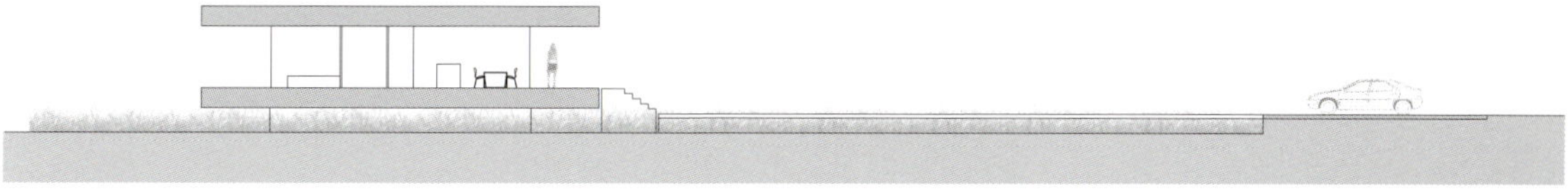

Section

Flag & Pole

Design
Ryuichi Ashizawa
Architects & associates

Location
Tokyo

Completion
2016

Area
529.2 square feet (49.16 square meters)

Photography
Kaori Ichikawa

Flag and Pole is a single-family residence and a clinic in the midst of the Dennenchofu residential area in Tokyo. The house is surrounded by similar-shaped sites where neighbors only build on the flag-shape portion of the lot, while the pole-shape section is left for entry and parking, leaving no room for a garden. In response to such a layout, the designer tried to make the most out of the site's distinctive character.

A design to maximize sun and wind exposure while adhering to local building restrictions resulted in a form that merged the 'flag' and 'pole' together. Inspired by the 'Garden City' concept, the flag-portion becomes a three-story architecture with space for a garden despite the limited space. Due to the irregular shape, all floors are able to receive adequate natural lighting and ventilation in the middle of a densely-populated area.

The clinic is located on the ground floor whereas the two floors above are dedicated to living spaces for the family. The living room, dining room, and kitchen on the second floor is connected to a terrace that cantilevers above the parking area.

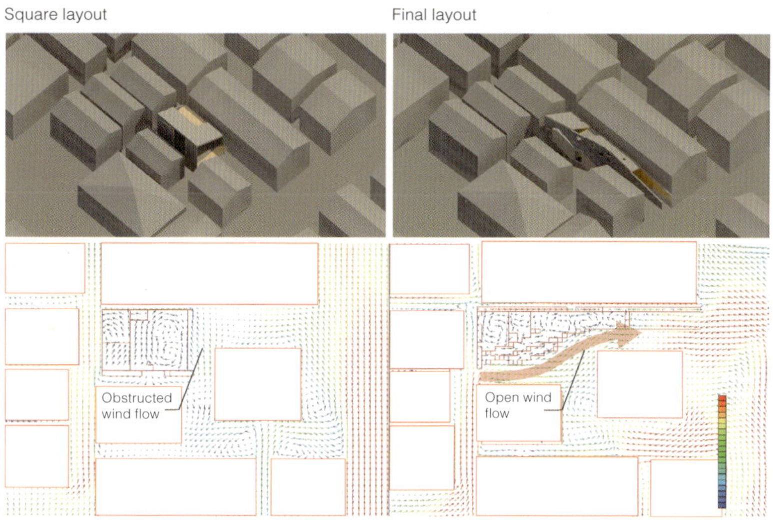

Wind analysis

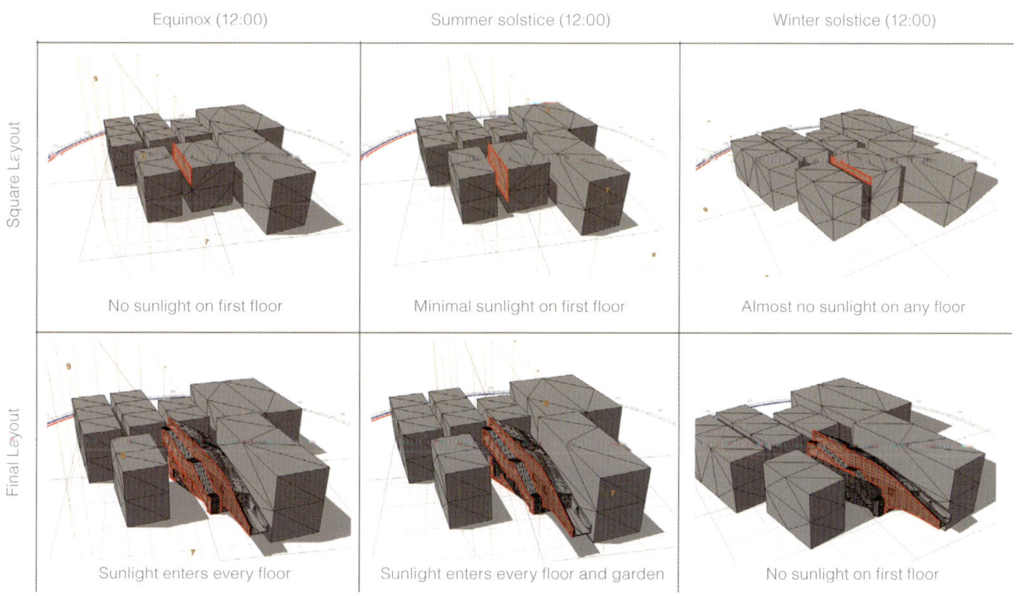

Sunlight analysis

Three-dimensional section

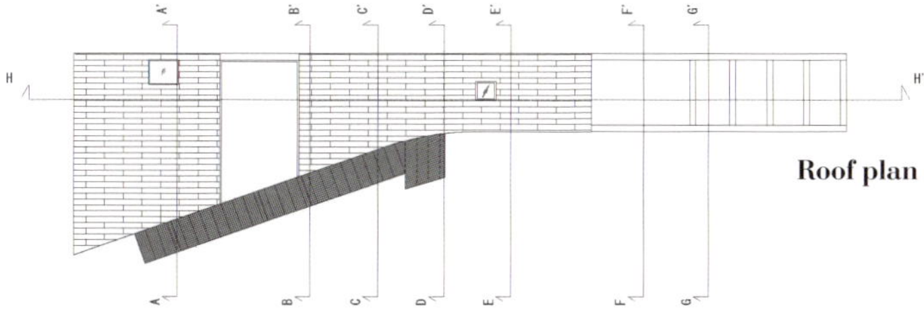

Roof plan

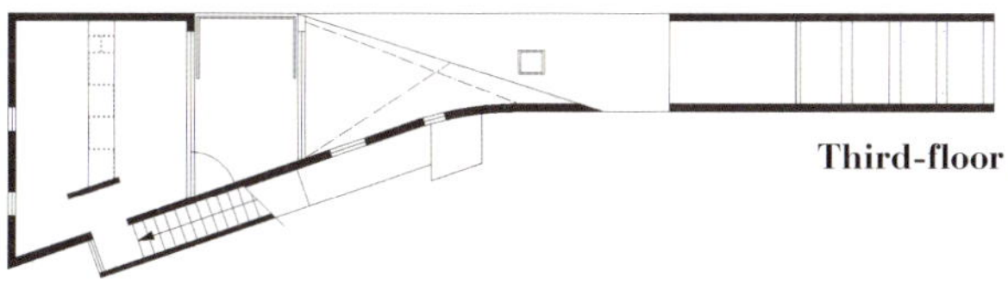

Third-floor plan

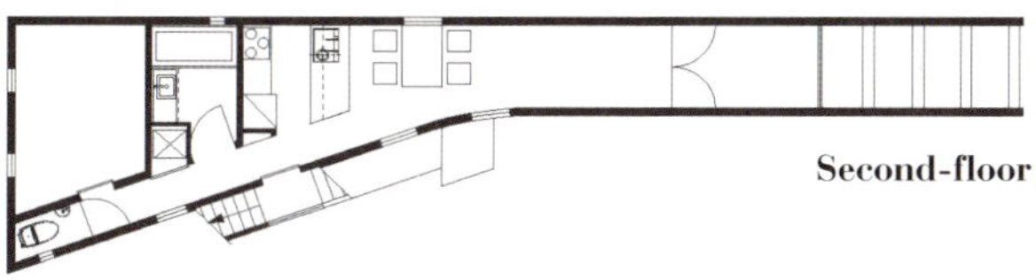

Second-floor plan

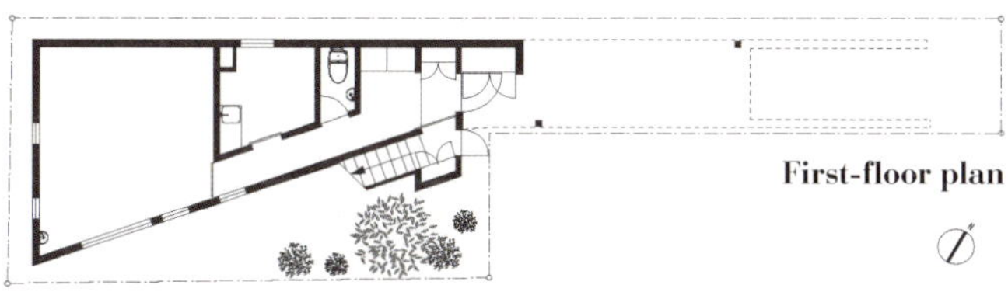

First-floor plan

Folding Roof House

Design
Ashida Architect & Associates

Location
Shibuya

Completion
2016

Area
912.7 square feet (84.79 square meters)

Photography
Satoshi Shigeta

The site is endowed with outstanding views, which were created by installing large openings and extended terraces. The purpose was to create a residence that would be able to reflect the urban street scenes. The building covers the maximum allowed space on the site, which is a corner lot with a broad width on a large road. Though the regulation on the set-back line was not rigorous, shading was carefully managed on account of regulation on building height. If the roof's design was made solely to tolerate the range of the shade regulation, it would be too stiff and unsuited for the scenic beauty of the top floor space. As a result, springing forth from the floor with the shape of cantilever, the roof slab was made using a folded-plate structure. The roof was designed to extend out into the scenery. Through repeated revisions, the designers ultimately found a shape to the roof that satisfied the two criteria mentioned above.

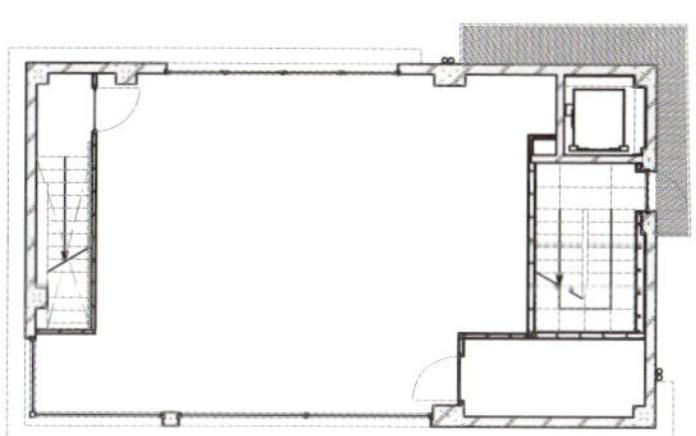

Second-floor plan

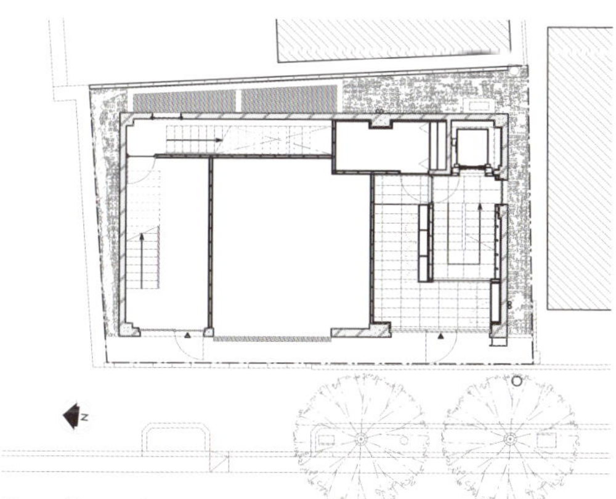

First-floor plan

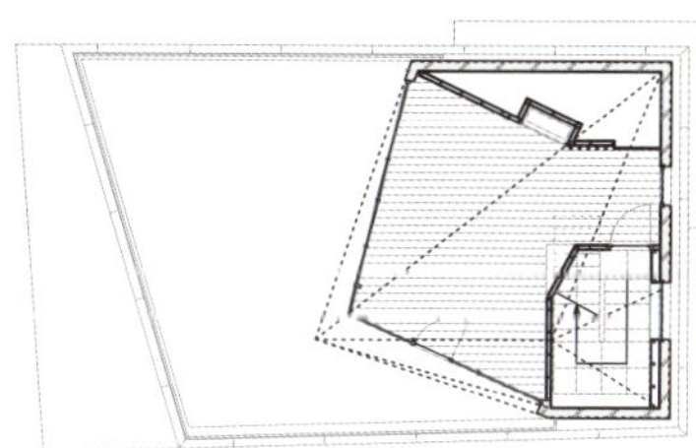

Fifth-floor plan

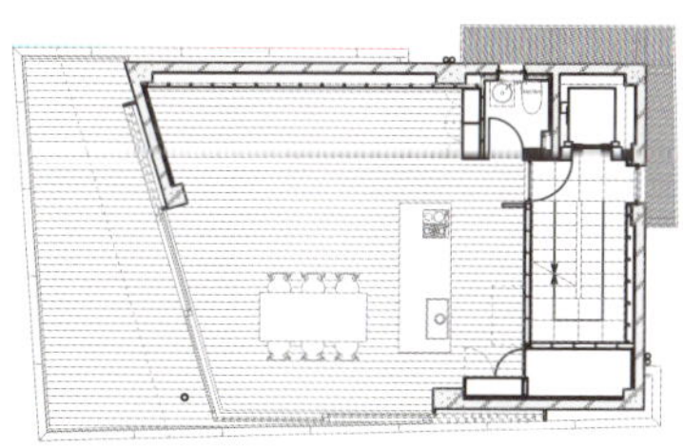

Fourth-floor plan

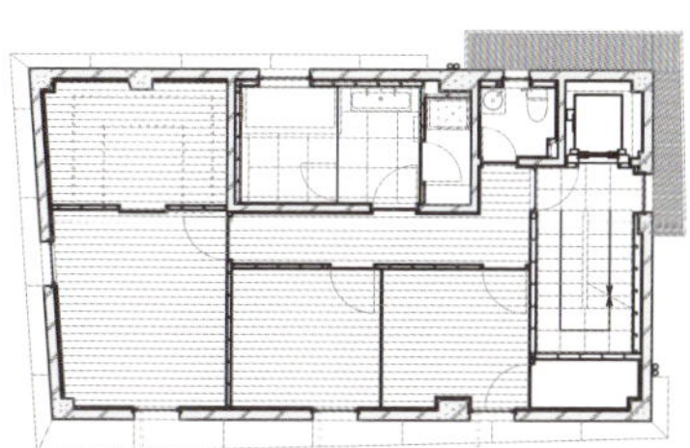

Third-floor plan

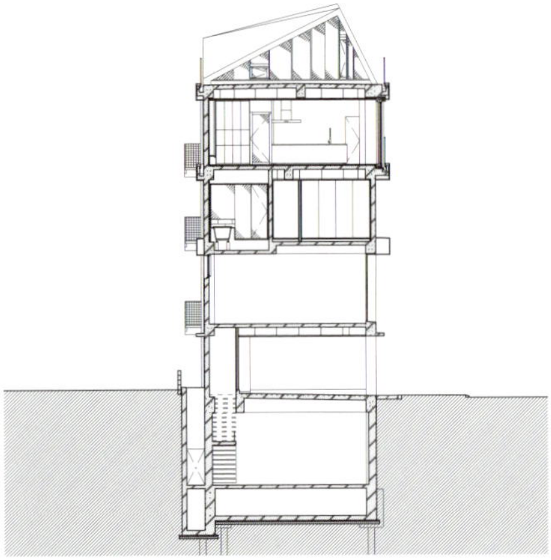

Cross section

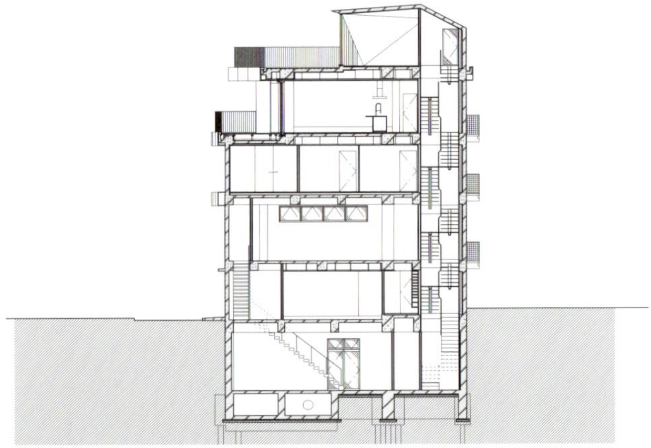

Longitudinal section

GO-BANG! House

Design
Takeru Shoji

Location
Nagaoka, Niigata

Completion
2014

Area
992.2 square feet (92.18 square meters)

Photography
Isamu Murai

On the first floor, four rooms—the master bedroom, a walk-in-closet, a Japanese-style room, and a spare room—are assembled as a compact core of day-to-day living and are placed in the center of the house. The core is surrounded with mortar flooring, playing an important role for the circulation and extension of activities.

The kitchen as well as the clients' favorite chairs were put in the attic on top of the small core, as if the living room was floating in the air. The outer roof is supported by three large suspended walls made with a steel truss and larch plywood with the same thickness as the outer wall. Thus, a spacious single room with large openings at the corner of the house is achieved. The spatial continuity between the inside and the outside is a result of the ambiguity created from the physicality of large plywood and the elaborate detailing of the opening.

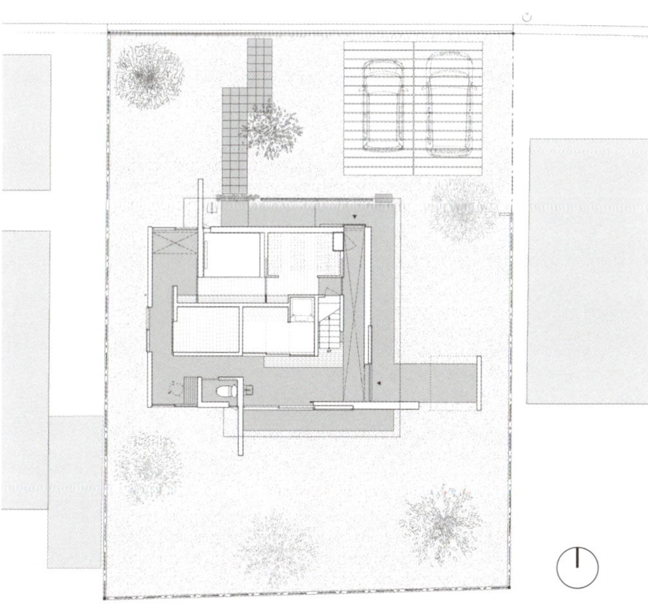

First-floor plan

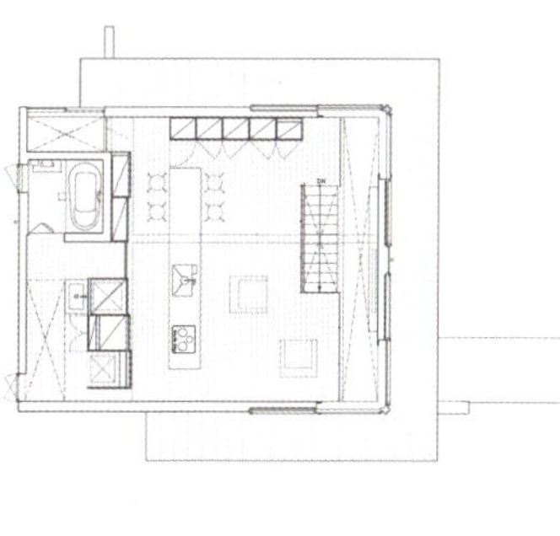

Second-floor plan

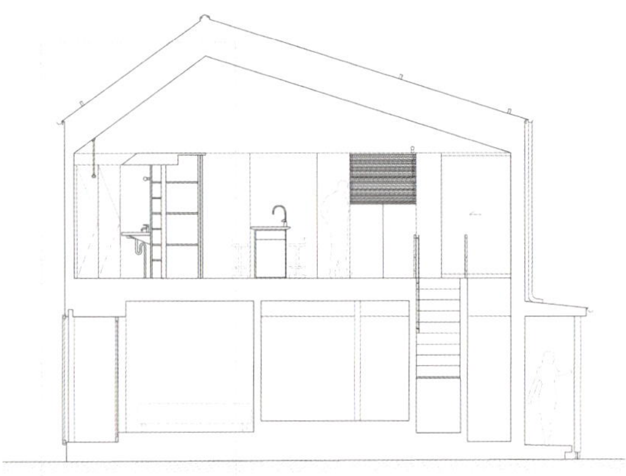

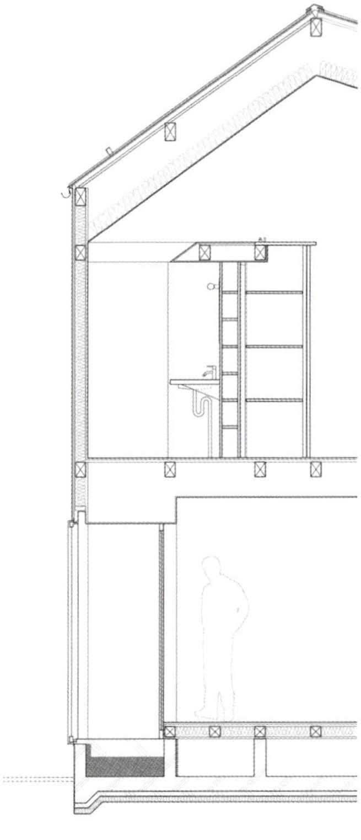

Section

Grigio

Design
Satoshi Kurosaki
(APOLLO Architects & Associates)

Location
Setagaya

Completion
2015

Area
670.8 square feet (62.32 square meters)

Photography
Masao Nishikawa

The L-shaped interior space around the courtyard is open and filled with natural light. The pleasant light from the courtyard illuminates the basement space. The basement has a bedroom for the clients' daughter and a second living room, where the family can relax.

The first floor has a main bedroom and storage areas as well as an open garage for two cars. The second floor has bathrooms and a living and dining room area that can be used to entertain guests. All rooms face toward the courtyard, in the interests of privacy. Diffused light from high windows and skylights formulates fine fluctuations in the gray scene. This living space, which resembles a small art museum in a city, also functions as a system to travel back and forth between the ordinary and extraordinary through the interaction with nature.

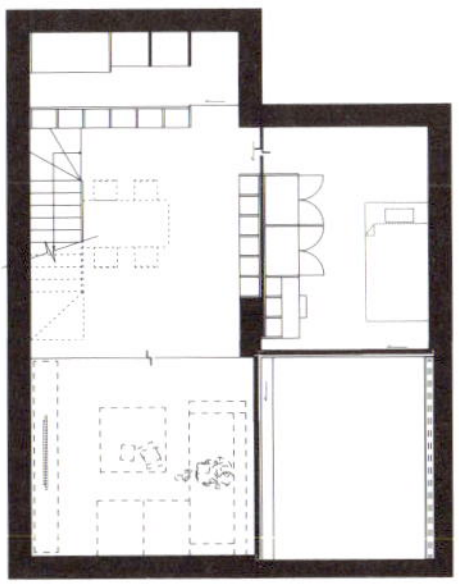

Basement plan

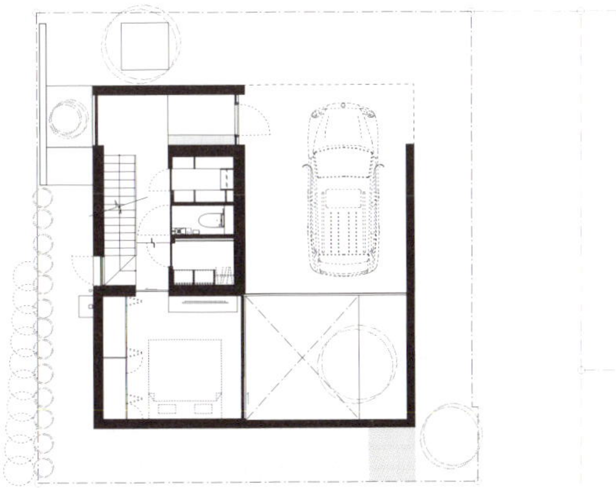

First-floor plan

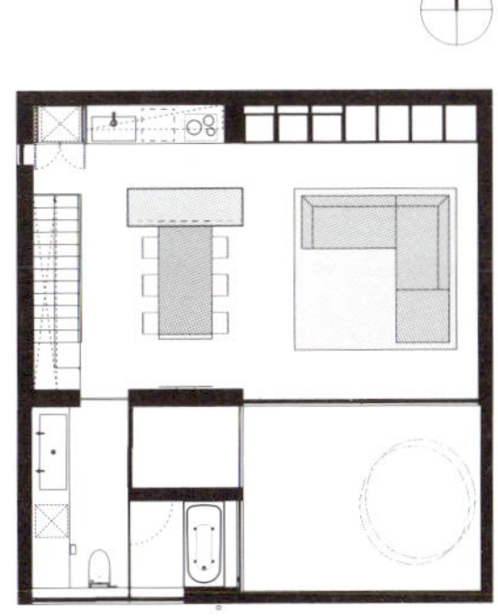

Second-floor plan

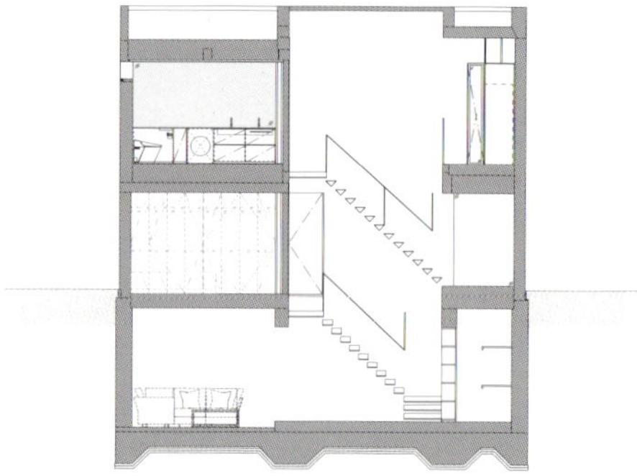

Section 1

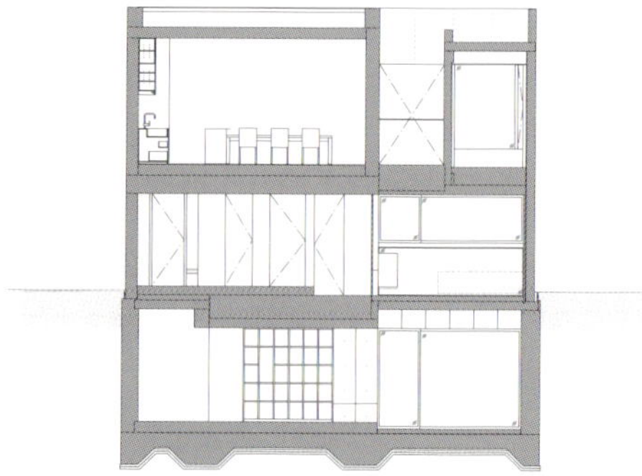

Section 2

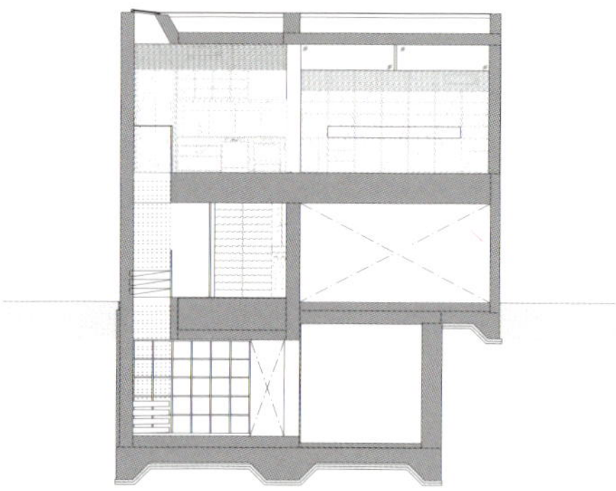

Section 3

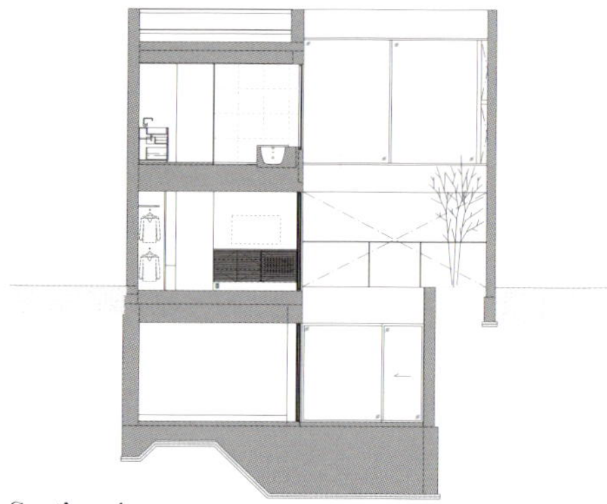

Section 4

Helix

Design
Shotaro Suga

Location
Osaka

Completion
2015

Area
3853.5 square feet (358 square meters)

Photography
Stirling Elmendorf

Beginning at the west-facing pond, the ground floor is open on approach, with wide openings that run from east to west. To increase openness and circulate air, the house is made from a continuous space from the pond through to the courtyard, towards the roof and following the southern surface at the penthouse. Light flows inside from the inner surfaces of the spiral layout. This space is supported by 42 evenly spaced pillars with a diameter of 2.4 inches (60 millimeters) each. To prevent from the heat bridge effect, wood was sandwiched between the pillars and enclosed with steel screens, with a tree planted in the center of the courtyard.

A composition that extends its environment into nature, and the precision of its construction, produces order and brilliance. Inspired by the universe beautifully balanced within life, the architects hope to recreate such experiences within spaces that are elevated against gravity, and filled with light.

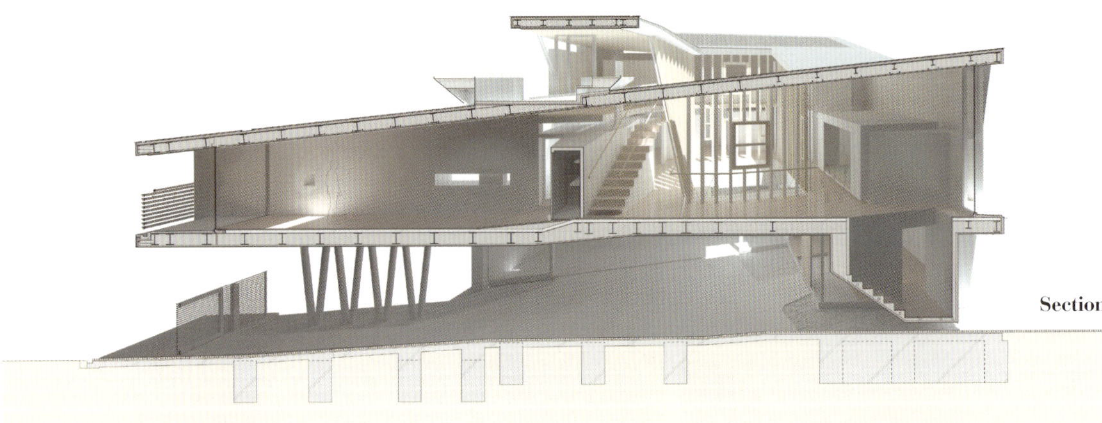

Section

Hex Tree House

Design
Shotaro Suga

Location
Nara

Completion
2015

Area
1539.2 square feet (143 square meters)

Photography
Stirling Elmendorf

This house is made of local Yoshino cedar. The frame is made of six asymmetrical sets of pillars and roof beams which are sandwiched between two diagonal sections. These roof beams of two different angles face each other, bound by a steel compression ring at the center.

On the first floor, There is a music room at the center, surrounded like an arena concert hall by the living room, dining, kitchen, and other areas. The south side is opened towards the green mountains, filling the space with light, breeze, and music. On the second floor, each room was placed around the central hall with a sky light. With this design, you can enjoy music in daily life as well as feel unity with the surrounding nature.

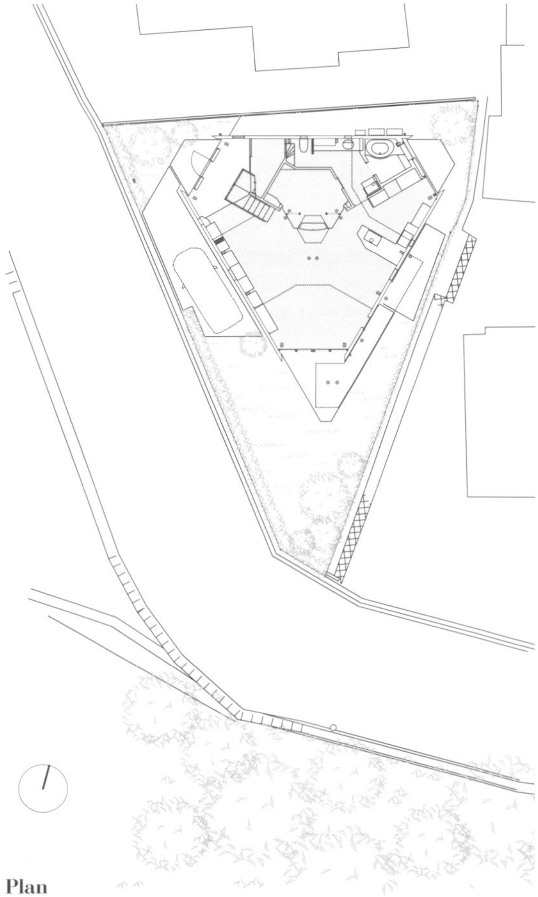

Plan

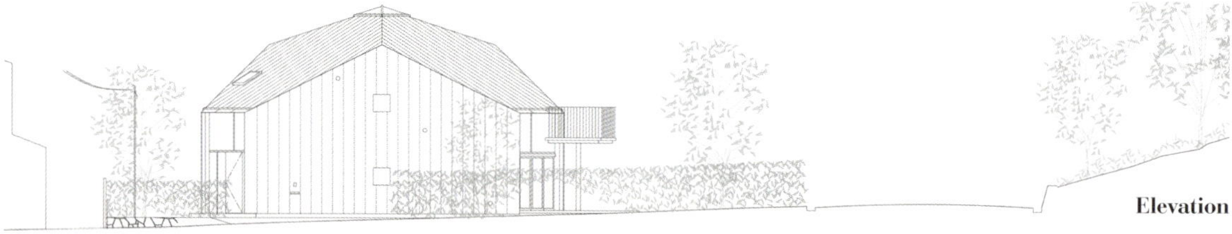

Elevation

House in Aonashi

Design
Sunao Koase, Ryota Yamagishi (SNARK), Shin Yokoo, Kakeru Tsuruta (OUVI)

Location
Maebashi

Completion
2017

Area
847.4 square feet (78.73 square meters)

Photography
Ippei Shinzawa

This project is a two-story residential building, located in the suburbs of Maebashi City. There are some thin rivers flowing at the foot of Mt. Haruna. Residential groups are scattered along the rivers. It is a beautiful landscape where rivers slip through between the fields and houses.

The architects thought of a residence integrated with the surrounding environment. The house consists of an elongated structure with three corners along the river. The roof has ridge lines to connect the vertices of each side so that it adjusts the scale of the whole, and also fits with the flow of the nearby river, the trees of Nakasu, and the mountains in the distance.

As a result, a garden was created, which is protected from the sun and the north wind outside and not separated from the surrounding environment. The interior was planned with an entrance, a kitchen and a living room together. These areas are loosely segmented by roof surfaces at different angles.

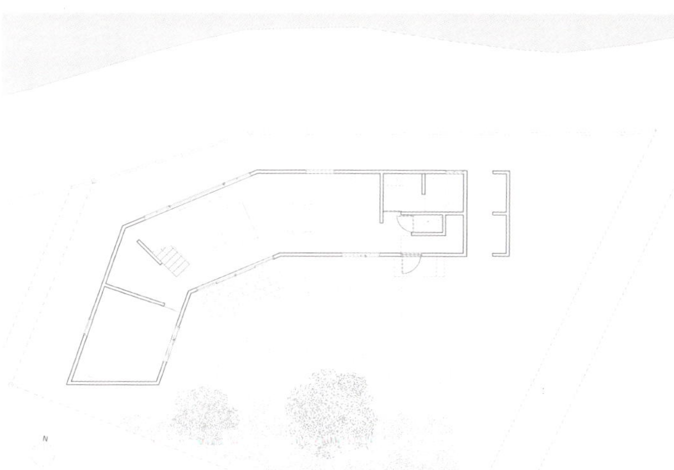

First-floor plan

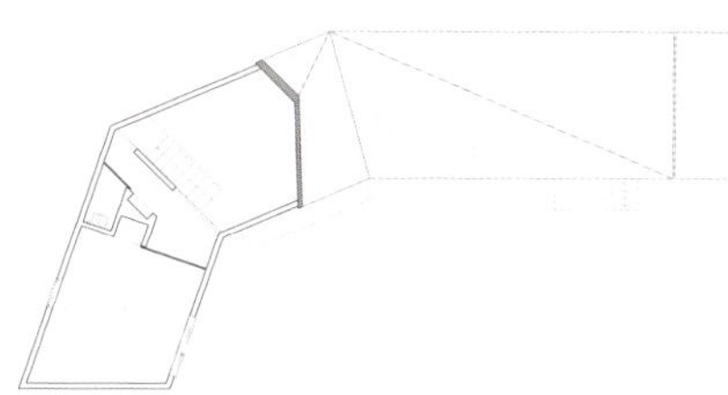

Second-floor plan

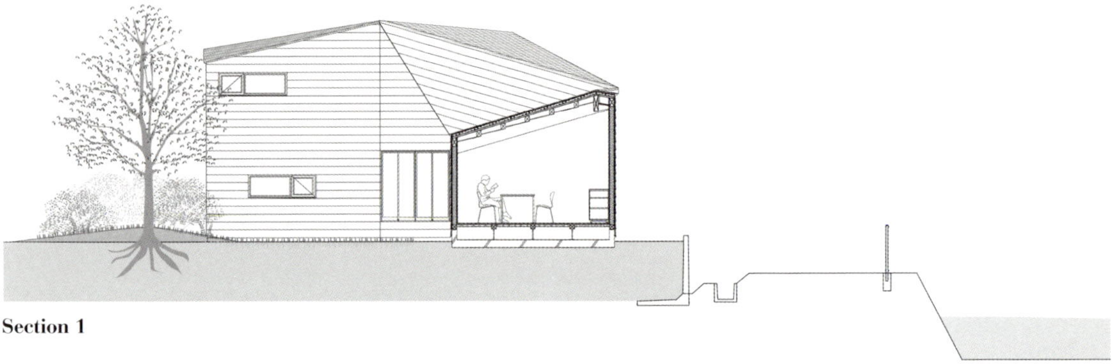

Section 1

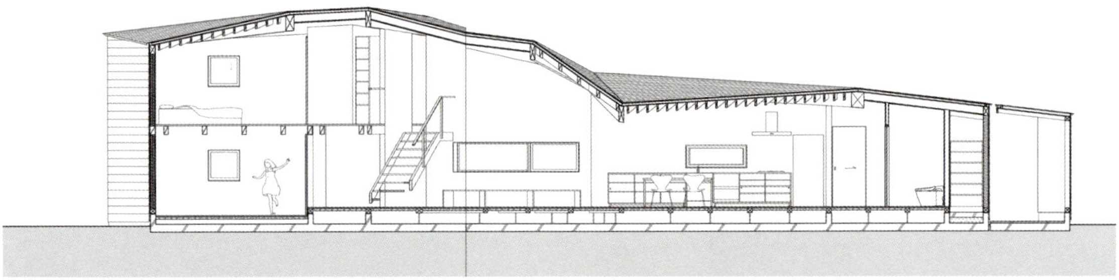

Section 2

House in Horikiri

Design
Masayoshi Takahashi, Sayoko Harada
(High Land Design)

Location
Katsushika, Tokyo

Completion
2014

Area
1190 square feet (110.55 square meters)

Photography
Atsushi Ishida

This project renovated a house built 40 years ago. Originally planning to place a living room on the first floor, the designers ultimately decided to place the living room on the second floor. A private room and a bathroom were placed on the first floor instead.

By carefully choosing the location of the stairs, the designers made it possible to allocate as much space as possible to the living room and dining room on the second floor. On the ceiling of the living room, a light was installed so that artificial lighting could be used with natural lighting. In addition, all the roof surfaces were made of glass, allowing even more light to come in. The designers transformed what was the darkest space in the house by encasing it in glass.

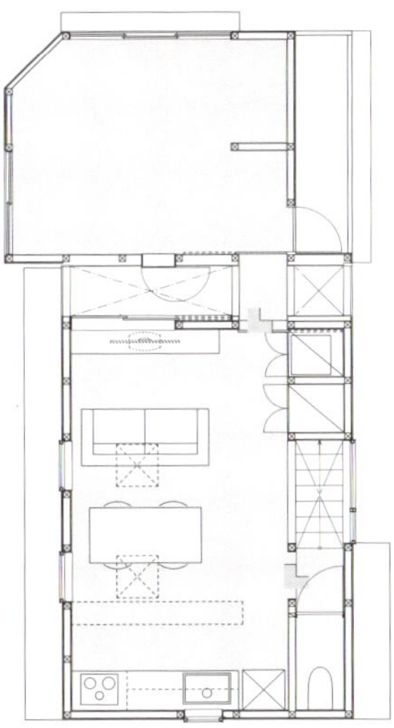

Second-floor plan

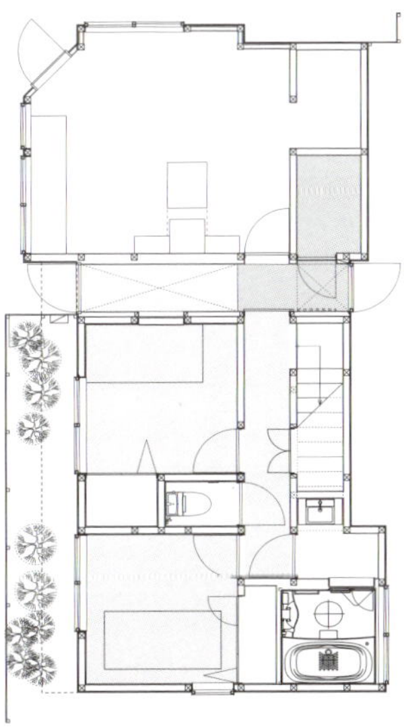

First-floor plan

House in Hoshigaoka

Design
Shogo Aratani Architect & Associates

Location
Hirakata-shi, Osaka

Completion
2016

Area
755.8 square feet (70.22 square meters)

Photography
Shigeo Ogawa

This is a project to design a small house for three adult residents—an elderly couple and their adult child. The first and second floors are layered in slightly shifted positions against each other, and a square roof is placed on top of those floors like an umbrella. The gaps produced by the shifted structures are turned into design elements, such as an open ceiling space. As a result, the layering of the lower floor and upper floor structures was carefully coordinated to define and adjust the dimensions of those elements. Finally, the depth of the eaves was defined in order to maximize the intake of daylight from the roof lighting.

The first-floor plan was set as a family gathering space and a space for the parents, while the second floor is the space for the single child, thus both levels have their own distinct style. However, each floor is connected through the open ceiling space so that each family member can feel each other's presence. This feature was also made in case the parents need special care in the future.

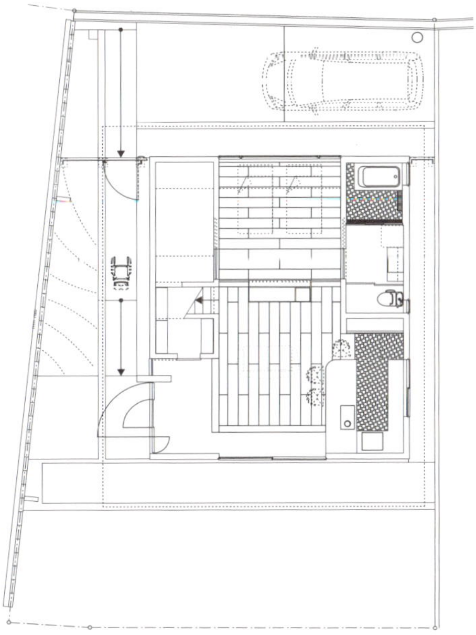

First-floor plan

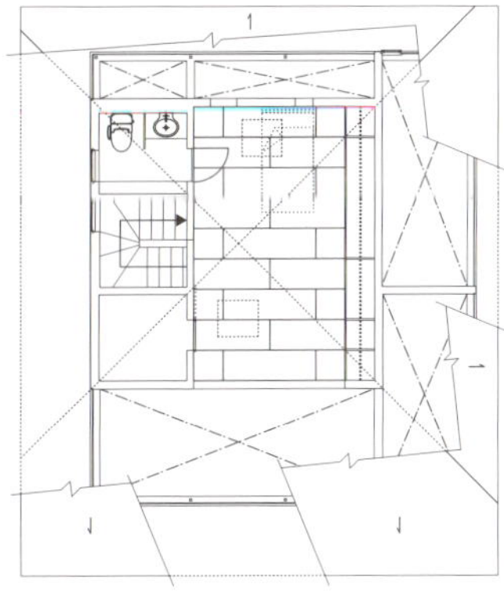

Second-floor plan

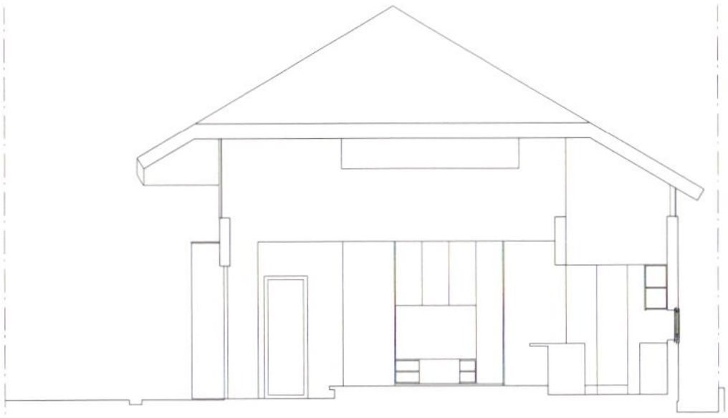

Section 1

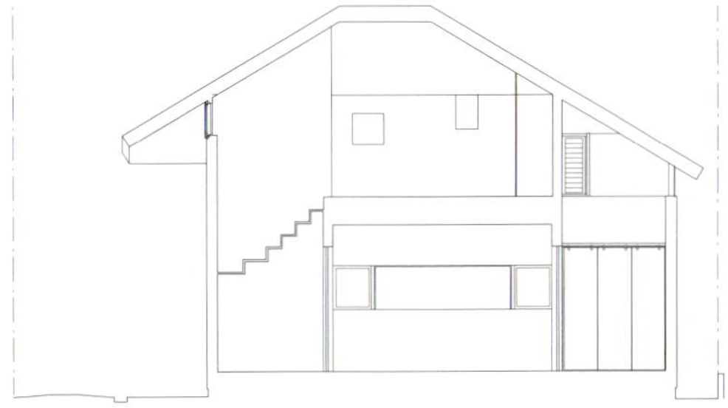

Section 2

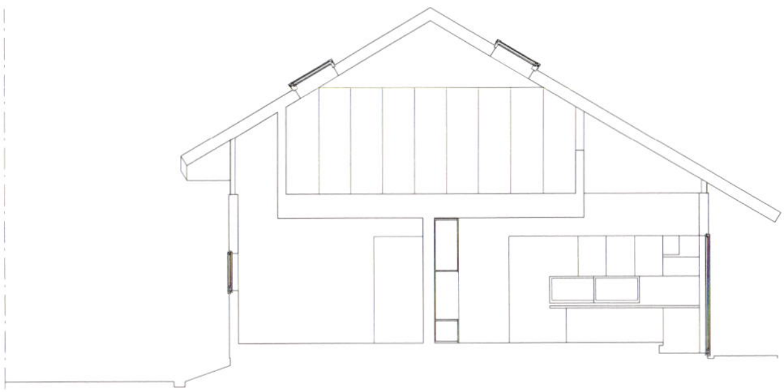

Section 3

House in Kichijoji

Design
Masayoshi Takahashi, Sayoko Harada
(High Land Design)

Location
Musashinoshi, Tokyo

Completion
2014

Area
846.7 square feet (78.66 square meters)

Photography
Atsushi Ishida

Producer
Style Labo

This is a project renovating a semi-commercial building to a residence.

Originally. there was a space on the first floor for a living area, kitchen and musical instruments, while on the second floor was the husband's atelier and the couple's bedroom. However, because the space has already been refurbished several times for different purposes, the space was in poor condition. The owners requested making the layout simple and reversing the composition of the first and second floors.

Therefore, the designers changed the position of the stairs greatly, giving a feeling of opening and bringing in light from the top of the stairs.

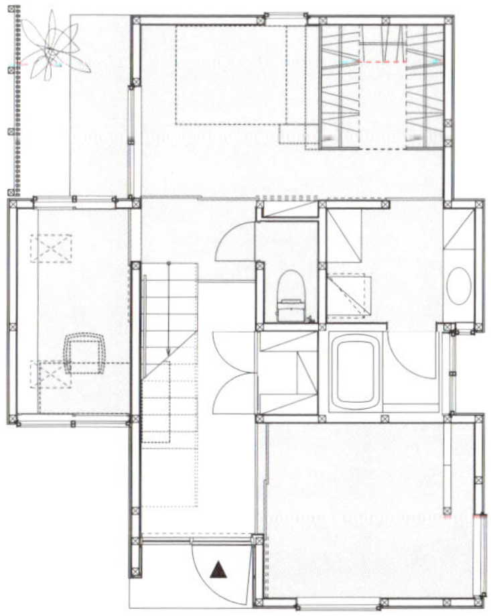

First-floor plan

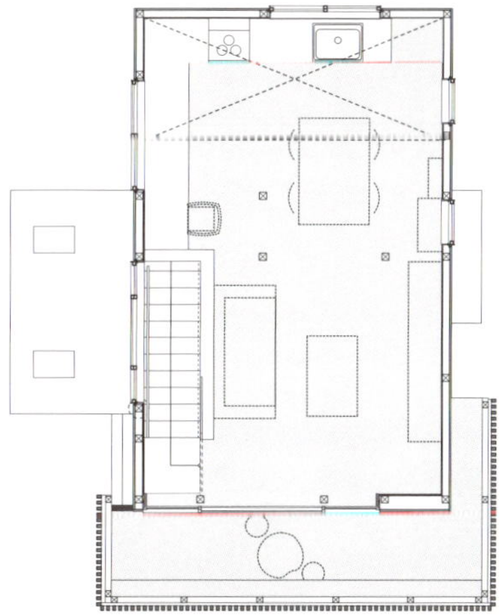

Second-floor plan

House in Kozenji

Design
Takanobu Kishimoto

Location
Hirakata, Osaka

Completion
2014

Area
694.3 square feet (64.5 square meters)

Photography
Eiji Tomita

The primary goal was that as soon you entered, you would feel relaxed because of the natural slope of the site. The entrance to the stairs has a deeper incline compared to the rest of the house. The height of the wall between the road and the house was increased to match the slope. The slope creates a difference in height equal about three floors. The partition of the space is reduced to the minimum, creating one large room with different functions distinguished by the difference in height and space. From the highest point, the family can gather together to use the space for different purposes.

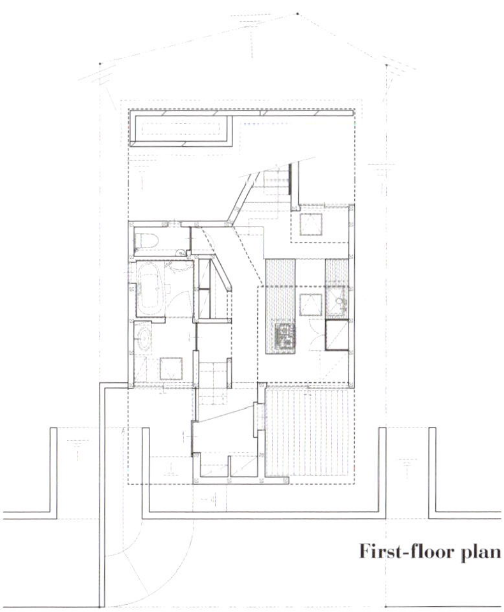

First-floor plan

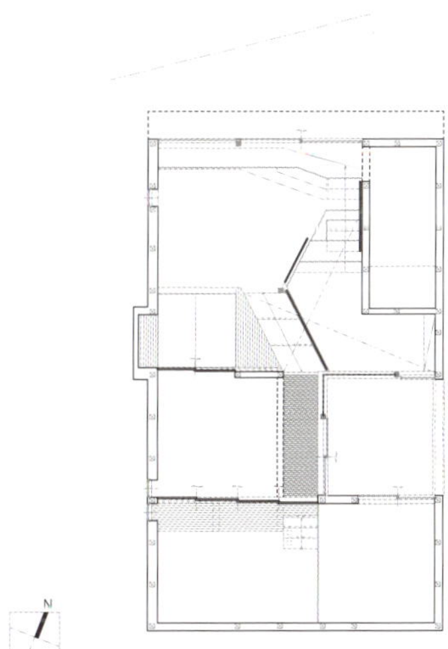

Second-floor plan

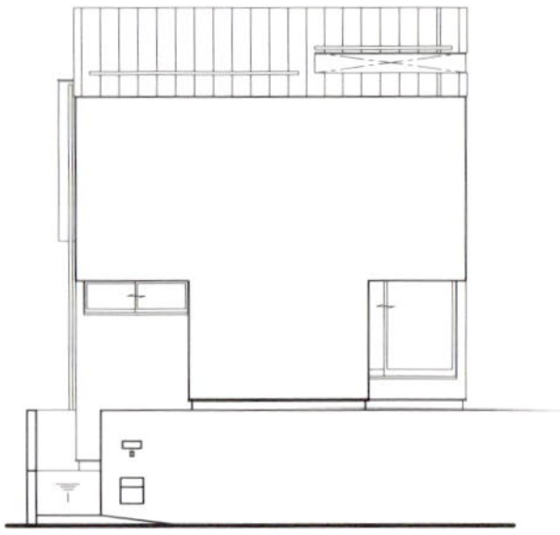

South elevation

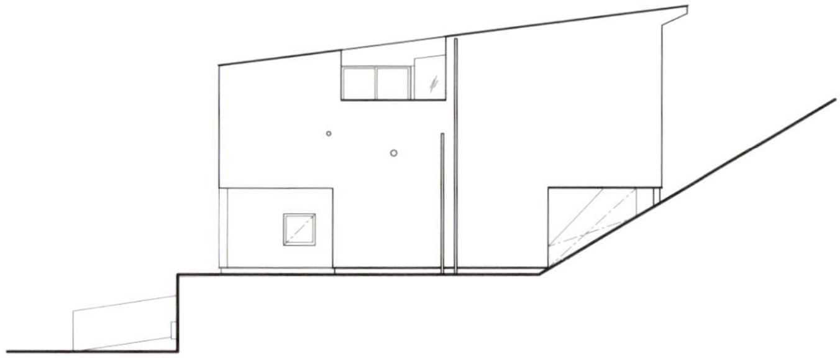

East elevation

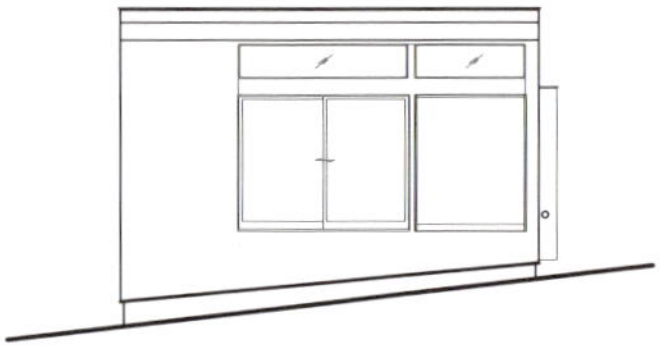

North elevation

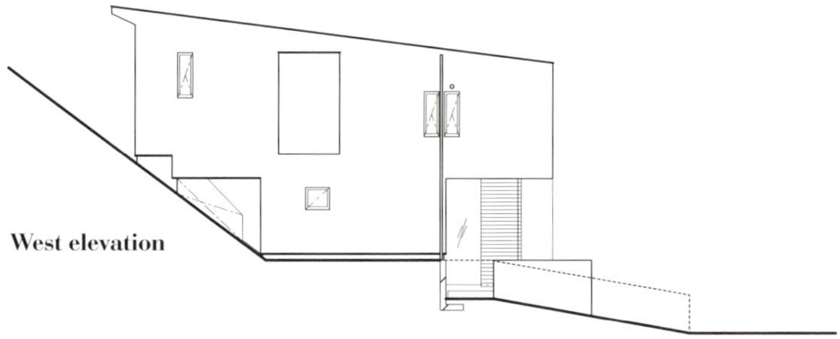

West elevation

House in Kyoto Nishijin

Design
Masato Sekiya

Location
Kyoto

Completion
2014

Area
1072.9 square feet (99.68 square meters)

Photography
Akira Kita

Four courtyard garden areas were created, with a total of five gardens, including the one at the back of the site. The west-side unit opens onto the street and has an entrance hall and a cloakroom downstairs. The central unit is the living room, which has a high ceiling for space and light. The third unit houses the dining room and kitchen, as well as a bathroom and laundry area with the parents' bedroom upstairs.

The three units' wooden sliding doors and fittings all have congruent positions on the first floor. Consequently, when they are all open, there is a view from the front entranceway to the courtyard. In addition, from the center of the living room, the east side of the garden and the rear of the site can be seen, creating a space reminiscent of Kyoto's traditional town. The hanging storage unit is covered in plaster, reflecting sunlight and artificial lighting, ensuring that there is a shower of light from above. Between the road in front and the entrance area is a long cobblestone path, surrounded by a lattice, expressing a traditional Kyoto image. This project maintains Kyoto's traditions while also exploiting architecture designs of the modern era.

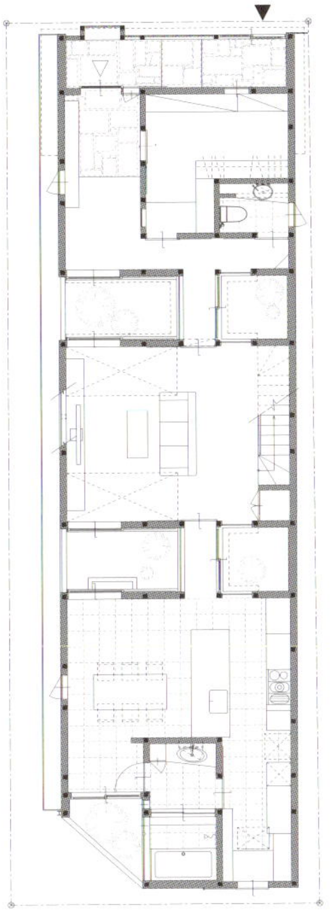

First-floor plan

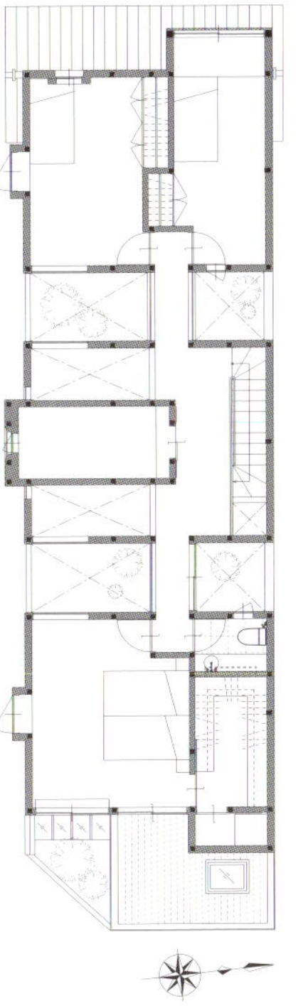

Second-floor plan

House in Nishino

Design
Yoshichika Takagi

Location
Sapporo, Hokkaido

Completion
2015

Area
1143.3 square feet (106.22 square meters)

Photography
Yuta Ooseto

The house is located on a residential area on a slope, near the center of Sapporo. Given the site has an irregular triangle shape, it was kept intact. The site has a height difference of about 13.1 feet (4 meters).

Building a foundation on such a slope is costly. The designer thought of making the excavation area for the foundation as small as possible. In order to cordon off enough space, they decided to protrude the second floor to make a separate building and set a terrace in the center of it. The wall of the second floor was slanted to make the volume larger. This would make the interior feel larger than it actually is. This also gives the terrace a house shape, making the terrace both an inner as well as an outer space.

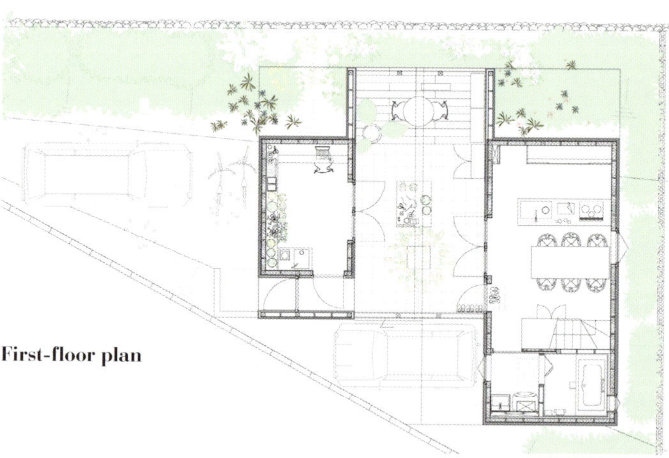

First-floor plan

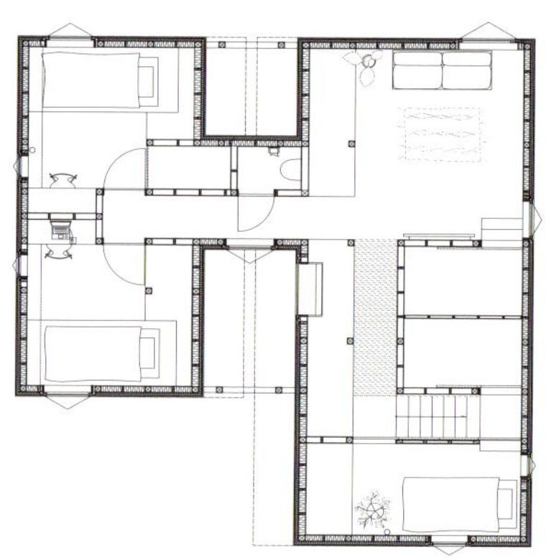

Second-floor plan

House in Sukumo

Design
Takanobu Kishimoto

Location
Sukumo

Completion
2017

Area
811.1 square feet (75.35 square meters)

Photography
Eiji Tomita

The first floor where everyone can enter is like an outdoor space, while the second floor is private space. Two rooms that are the same size were placed on the both sides of the courtyard on each floor. The designer didn't set up a specific usage of these rooms and planned for these rooms to adapt to changing needs in the future.

Since the open space is exposed to wind and rain, the designer opened a square aperture in the roof of the courtyard to let wind escape. The wind hitting the building is channeled through the courtyard to the upper part of the building.

The first floor is like an outdoor space. Thus, natural stones were chosen as the floor's finishing material. The second floor is a private space for the family, making cedar boards a suitable finishing material for the floor, bringing extra warmth to the space. By using different materials for the first floor and second floor, different atmospheres are created.

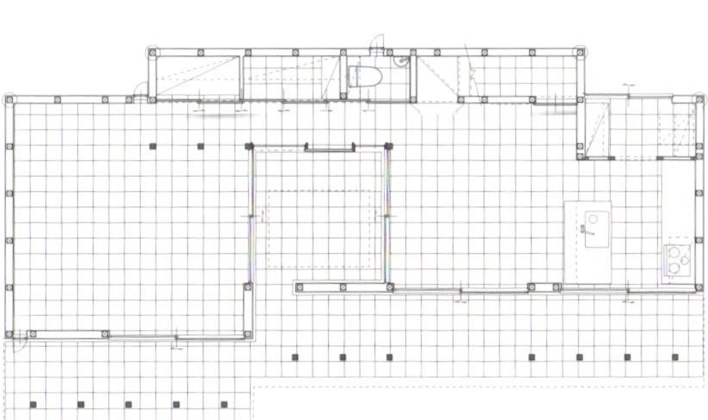

First-floor plan

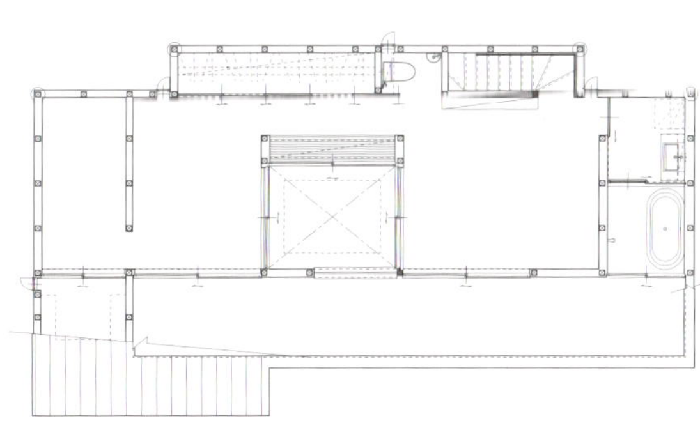

Second-floor plan

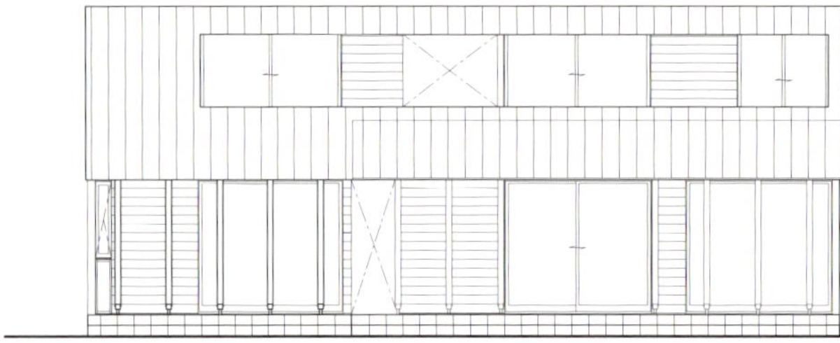

South elevation

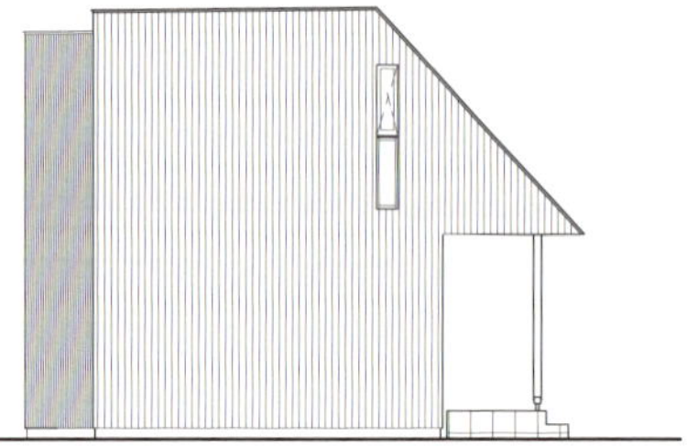

West elevation

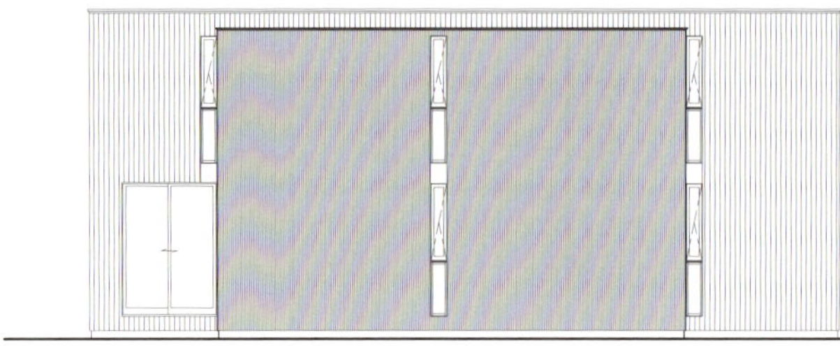

North elevation

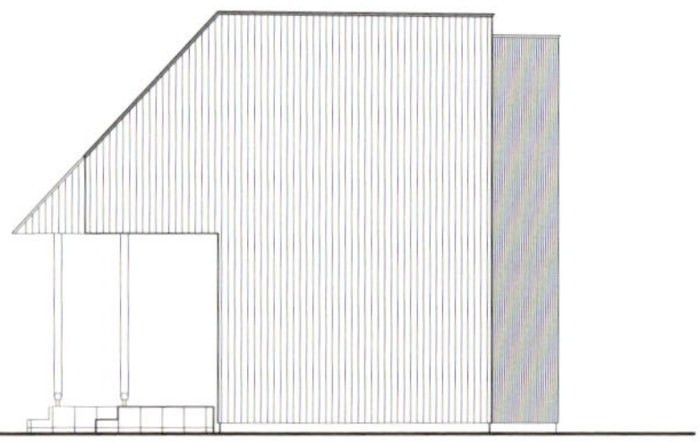

East elevation

にんじん
あーんあん

House in Wakabayashi

Design
Hiroto Suzuki Architects and Associates

Location
Miyagi

Completion
2017

Area
934.8 square feet (86.85 square meters)

Photography
Studio Monorisu

This house is located in a residential area in Sendai. Rebuilt old houses are scattered. Therefore, old and new houses are mixed around there. The house is surrounded by other houses, and the neighboring houses are closely built to the property's boundary.

As a result, the architects' concept was to make a generous connection between the private and public areas to easily interact with the neighborhood. The architects planned a three-story building and an outdoor space for parking and gardening. To create a place for gatherings, the designers placed the living, dining, and kitchen areas on the second floor as a public space for family and guests. Immediate access to the living, dining, and kitchen areas from outside via a terrace and staircase creates a gradual connection to the community.

The neighboring buildings are planned with a perpendicular grid from the front road, facing the adjacent house. The architects decided to situate the building at a 45 angle from the front road. As a result, the view is not interrupted by neighboring buildings, and the interior gets additional sunlight.

First-floor plan

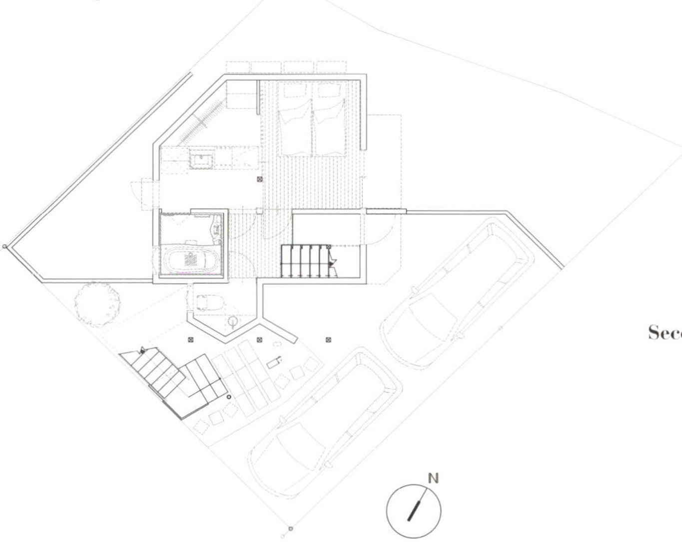

Third-floor plan

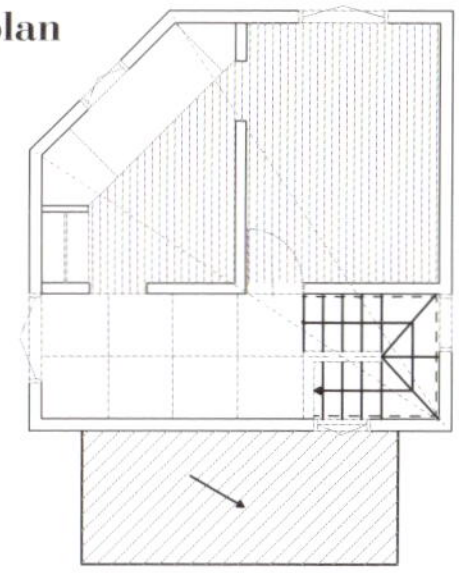

Second-floor plan

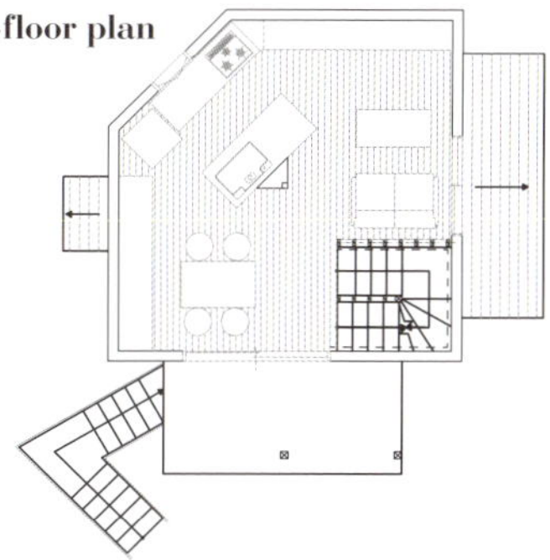

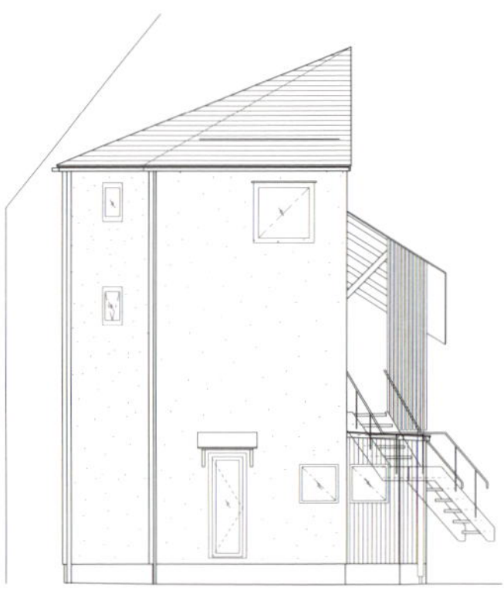

West elevation

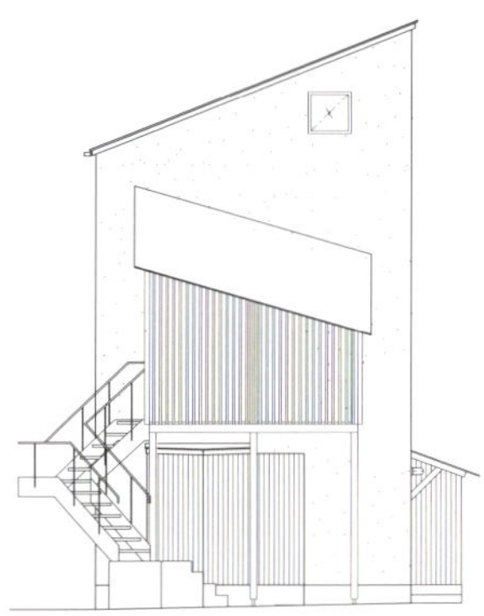

South elevation

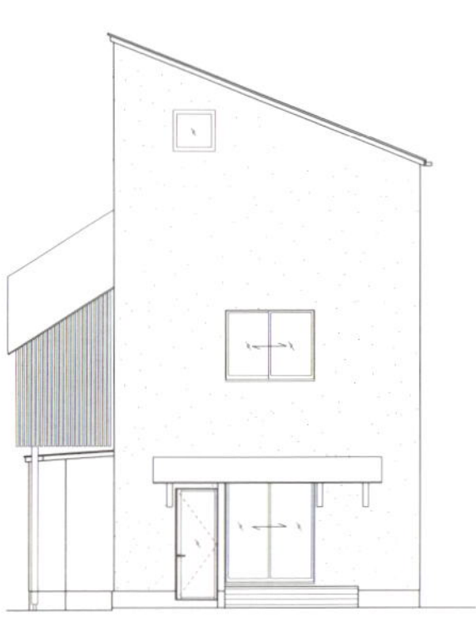

East elevation

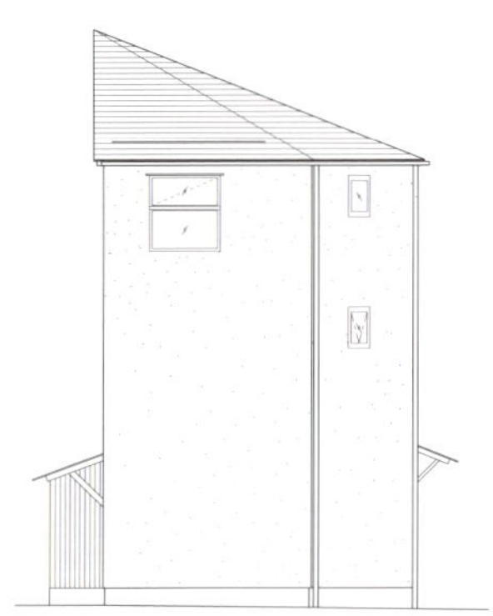

North elevation

House M

Design
Asai Architects

Location
Yokohama

Completion
2016

Area
430.6 square feet (40 square meters)

Photography
Asai Architects

This is a wooden two-story residence in the residential part of Yokohama city. The pillars are Japanese cypress, the beams pine, and the second floor uses J panels, which are a laminated material often used for construction and furniture made from Japanese cedar. In addition to the aforementioned construction materials, the house is designed using a combination of various types of wood. The first floor is finished with mild woods, such as Japanese red pine and Japanese linden, while the second floor utilizes rich woods, such as kempas.

As far as the floor plan is concerned, the first floor has a barrier-free layout with sliding doors in various locations. This way, the space can be used as either an integrated or a divided space, depending on one's needs. The second floor has exposed beams and is laid out as a single room. Either a large walk-in closet or a bathroom can be built underneath the lofted area.

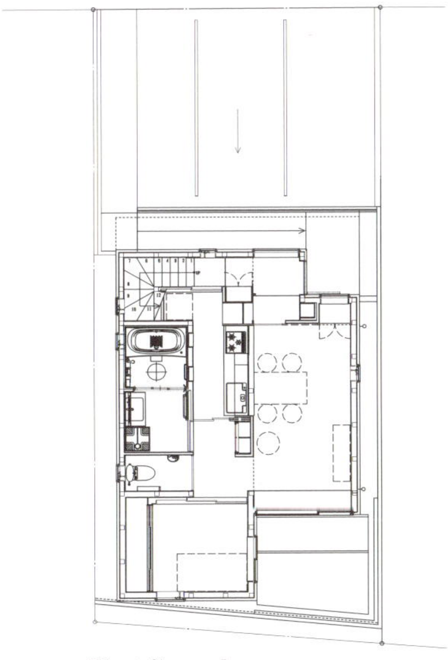

First-floor plan

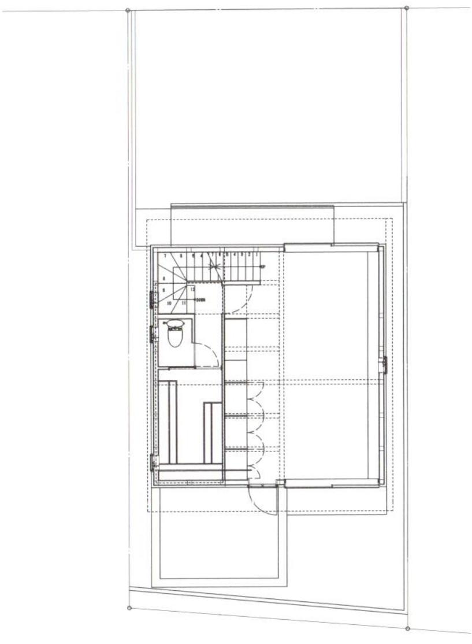

Second-floor plan

House in Suwamachi

Design
Kazuya Saito Architects

Location
Miyagi

Completion
2016

Area
1163 square feet (108.05 square meters)

Photography
Yasuhiro Takagi

Since the environment is busy and noisy, the designer considered creating a comfortable residential environment. The high-ceiling entrance and staircase are designed as a buffer space that can control not only light and wind from the outside, but also noise as well. The structure consists of two layers with a master bedroom, kitchen, living and dining rooms as well as another bedroom and a loft. Compared to the bare-framed roof, the interior is organized with partitions of white gate-type walls so that the space can change in appearance from room to room. They had realized a continuous spacial composition by a gradual connection to outside through a buffer space, while securing the independence of each room.

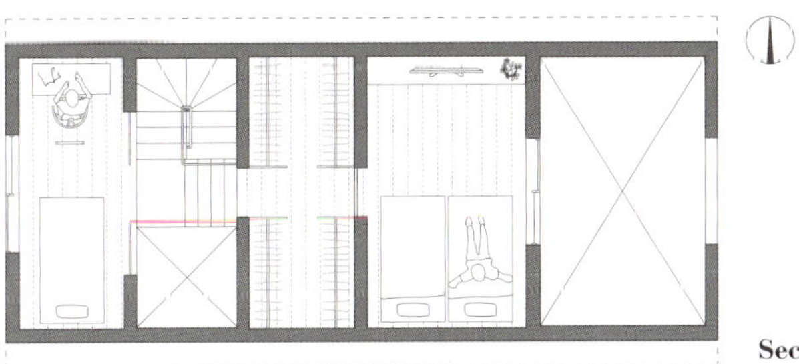

Second-floor plan

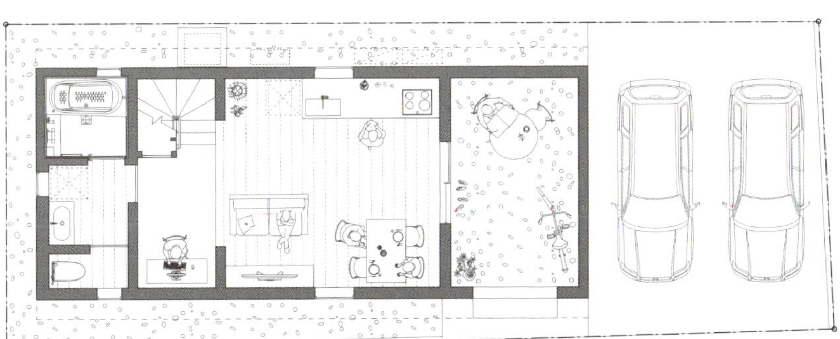

First-floor plan

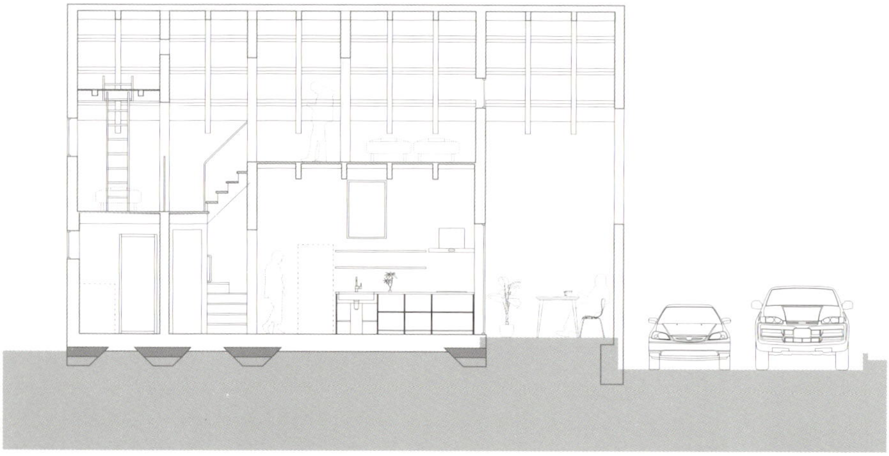

Section

House with a Square Roof

Design
Katsutoshi Naoi, Noriko Naoi
(Naoi Architecture & Design Office)

Location
Yamagata

Completion
2014

Area
2846.5 square feet (264.45 square meters)

Photography
Hiroshi Ueda

The clients requested a playful home that would make life indoors during the long winter more fun. The designer responded by proposing a layout in which split levels and creative circulation routes would connect the rooms in a complex but systemic network. This freeing of interior space made daily life more fun, however, it also had to coexist with an exterior whose atmosphere and appearance was respectful of the long-established surrounding streetscape.

In order for the house to blend in with this streetscape, it has a simple pyramid hip roof and is sunk partially underground, which retains the volume by keeping the height to 4.9 feet (1.5 meters) above ground. The house includes a courtyard that serves as a symbolic site for daily interaction with nature and year-round observation of the changing seasons. A wood stove provides primary heating for the fully open and interconnected interior. The design does not simply encourage the residents to stay inside comfortably during winter, but also emphasizes the metaphorically warm lifestyle through the act of gathering around the stove's flames, an activity only possible because of the cold winters in the local area.

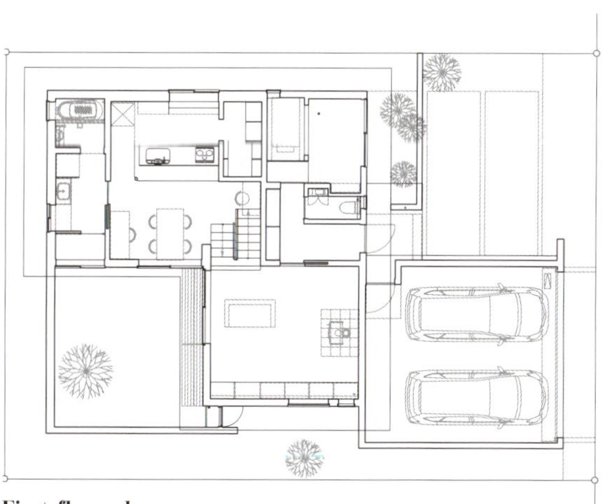

First-floor plan

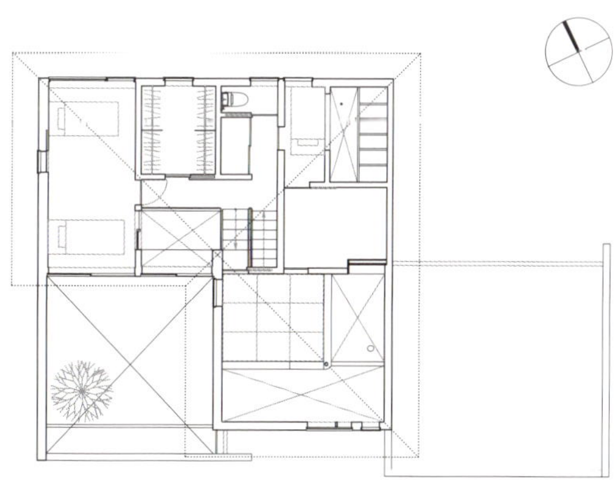

Second-floor plan

Kokonoma House

Design
Takanobu Kishimoto

Location
Maizuru, Kyoto

Completion
2014

Area
1007 square feet (93.57 square meters)

Photography
Eiji Tomita

The client wanted a pleasant home with plenty of sunlight. The designers chose a square space with the length of 17.7 feet (5.4 meters) and installed an S-shaped roof. The rest of the space connects to an atrium, allowing sunlight to shine in from the south. Four lattices with the length of 8.9 feet (2.7 meters) come together to form this square space. People can feel the unity between the interior and the exterior, receiving sunlight from the south via the roof slope.

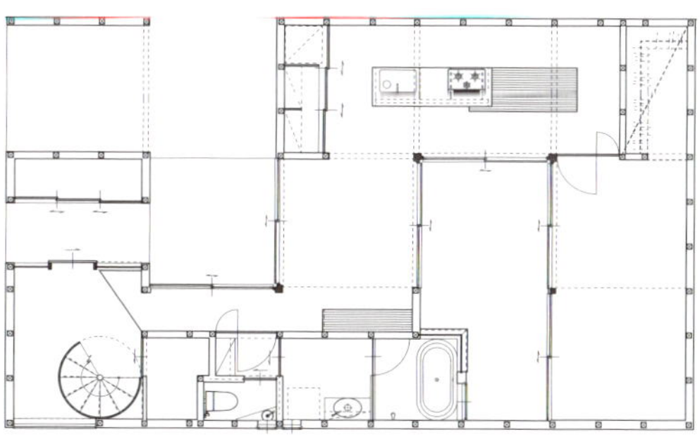

First-floor plan

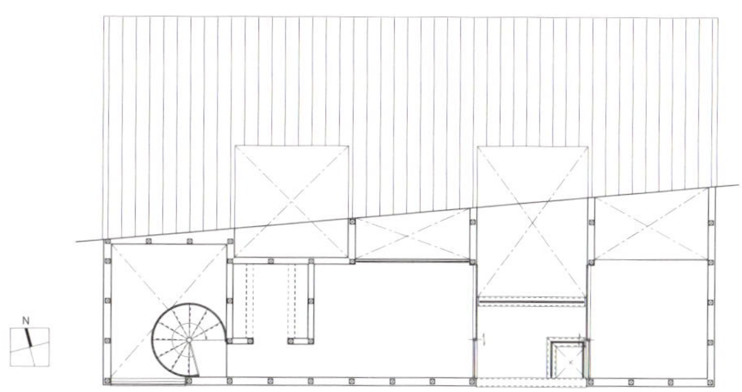

Second-floor plan

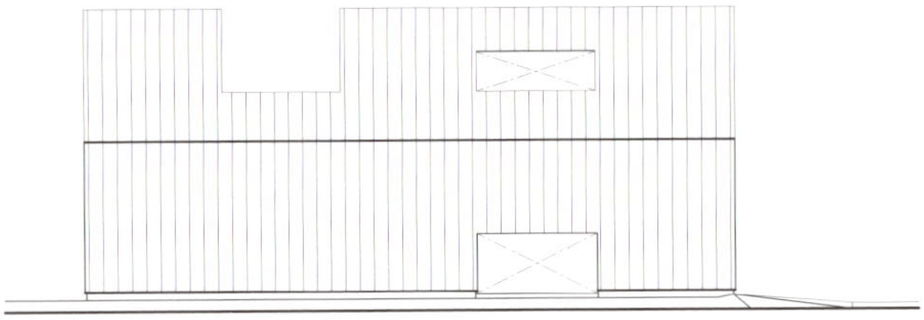

North elevation

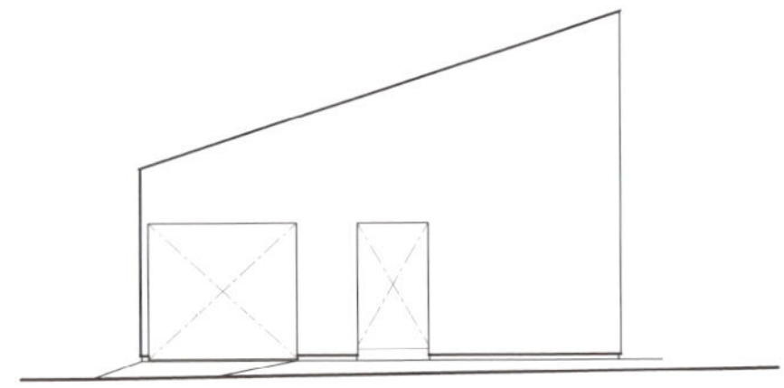

West elevation

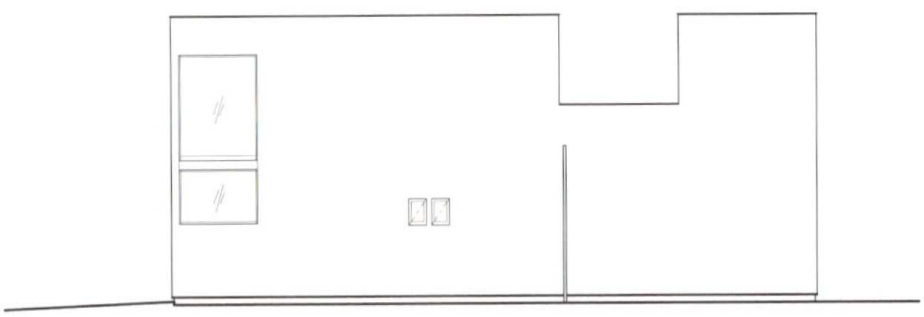

South elevation

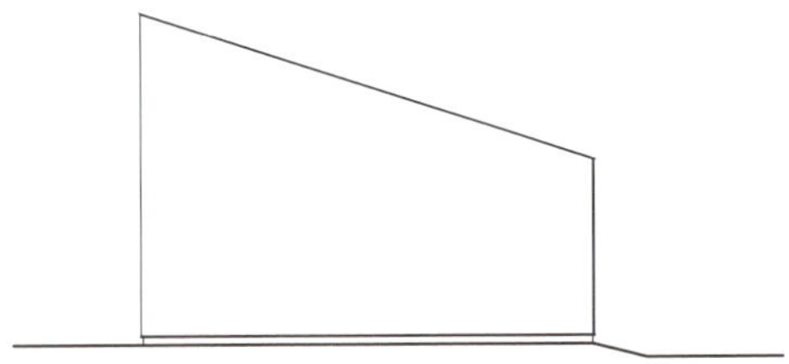

East elevation

Lakeside House

Design
Shinichi Ogawa & Associates

Location
Yamanashi

Completion
2015

Area
1914.9 square feet (177.9 square meters)

Photography
Shinichi Ogawa & Associates, Toshiyuki Yano

The site is located in an attractive location facing a lake. The surface of a lake glistens and appears to move with wind. Also, there are a big zelkova and a Japanese maple.

The longitudinal side of the structure faces parallel to the lake in order to provide a full view of the lake from all the rooms. The interior has a simple plan. The space, without any decorative elements, confronts nature. The interior space is filled with natural light and the color outside changes over the course of the day.

This architecture creates a wonderful, refreshing place filled with plenty of nature, from the soothing light in the morning to the reflections off of the lake.

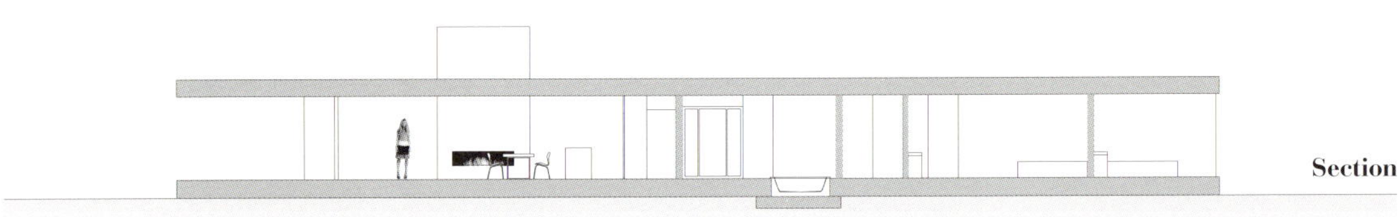

Section

Plan

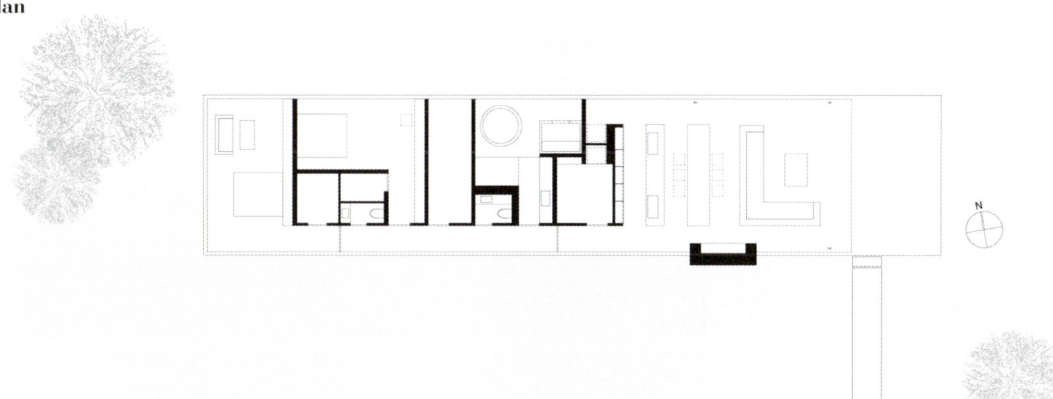

Light Well House

Design
KINO architects (Masahiro Kinoshita)

Location
Tokyo

Completion
2015

Area
511.8 square feet (47.55 square meters)

Photography
Kai Nakamura

This house was constructed for a young couple and their child. For a high-density residential area, they needed privacy, sunlight, and openness in the house. This house is designed with a 'light well' that linked to the terrace and staircase, creating a continuous vertical connection. The spacious volume, by creating a buffer zone between the external and internal space, guides light and wind into the interior, adding to the sense of openness. The aim was to connect the inside with the outside by stacking the space instead of installing too many windows.

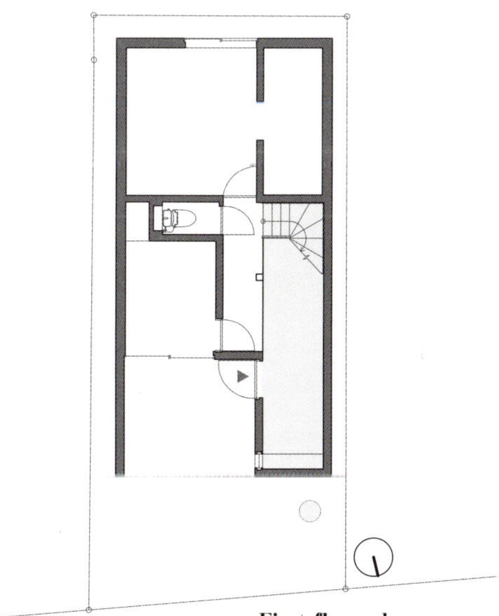

First-floor plan

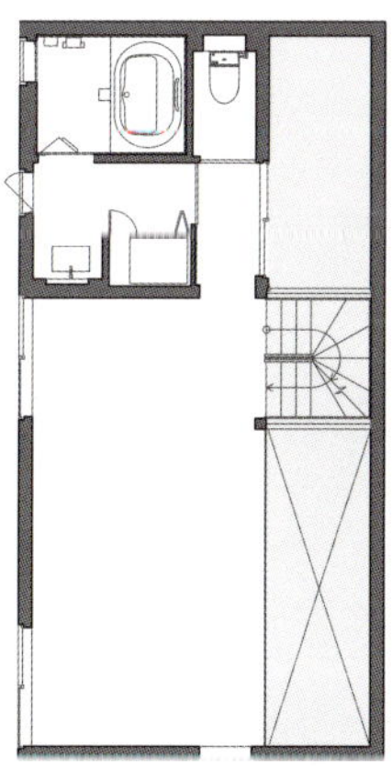

Second-floor plan

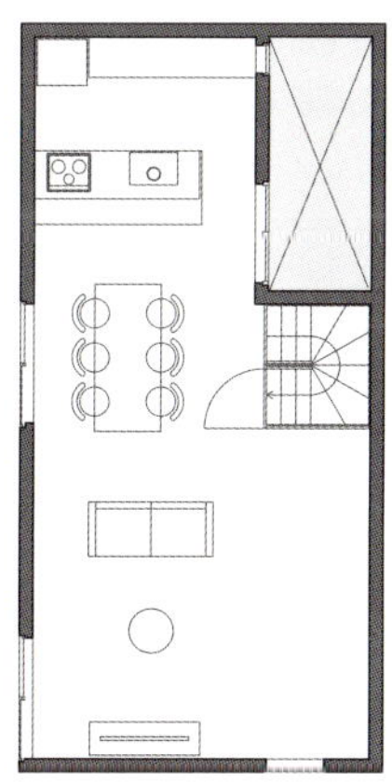

Third-floor plan

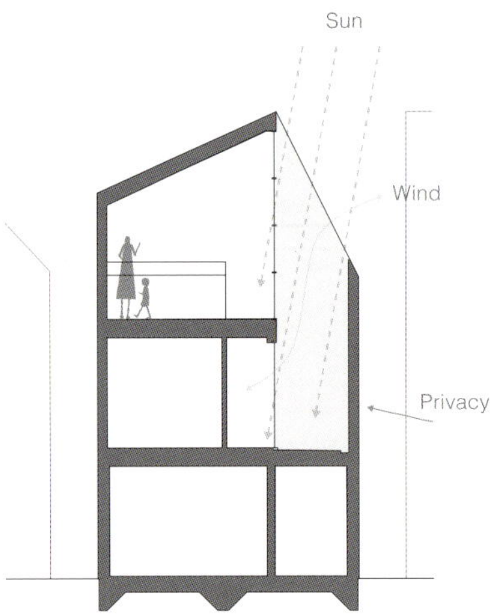

Section 1

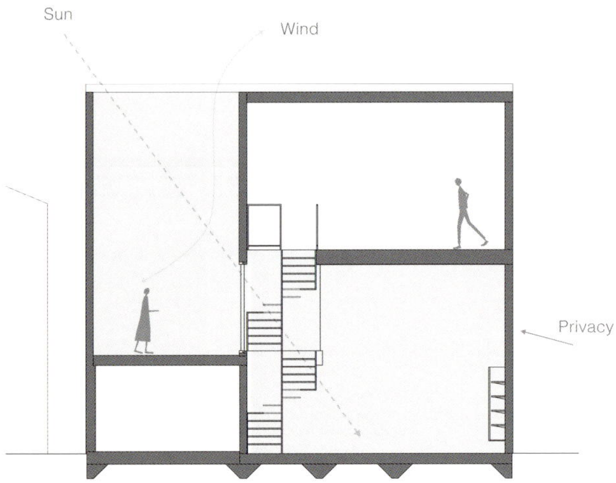

Section 2

Link

Design
studio LOOP

Location
Gunma

Completion
2014

Area
516.3 square feet (47.97 square meters)

Photography
Kai Nakamura

The designer intended to make a high-end residence that was environmentally friendly and inexpensive to offset the budget on purchasing the land. In addition, there was also the goal of leaving room for potential expansion in the future.

A highly hygroscopic tile was used on the inner wall, and a gradation blind for the windows reflects natural light towards the ceiling, which has a highly reflective finish, adding extra light to the space. The future children's room can be created by adapting pre-existing rooms of the parents' when necessary. As part of designing for a suburban area, it is important not only to protect the environment and reduce costs by making good use of available resources, but also to create the environment where children can spend time with their grandparents.

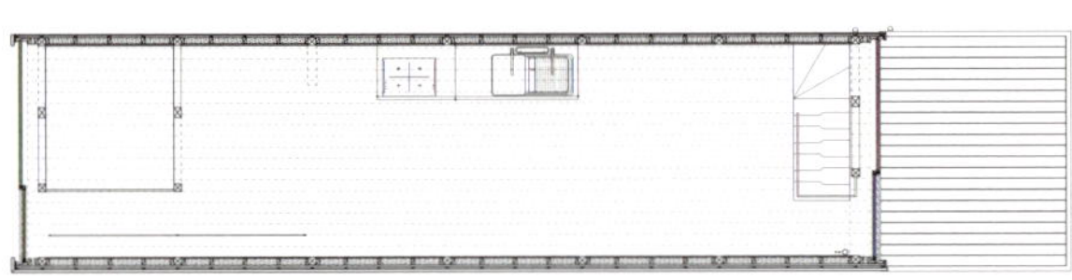

Second-floor plan

First-floor plan

M House

Design
Masayoshi Takahashi, Sayoko Harada
(High Land Design)

Location
Koganei, Tokyo

Completion
2015

Area
1164 square feet (108.14 square meters)

Photography
Atsushi Ishida

The designers decided to place the private areas of the house, such as the bedroom, on the first floor and make the living room, a dining room, and kitchen as a one-room space on the second floor, making the house as spacious as possible. By raising the ceiling height of the living room area, the loft was secured as a storage space. By making the opening of the high side of the same height as the ceiling height of the loft large, an opening feeling was created while securing the necessary walls for doing housework such as kitchen.

The kitchen is located on the north side of the second floor. Green springs out from the big window behind, with a black tile on one side of the wall. The surface material is oak. Thus the stainless steel plating for the counter is extra thin. The kitchen has carefully planned organization, allowing the owners to cook with ease and enjoyment.

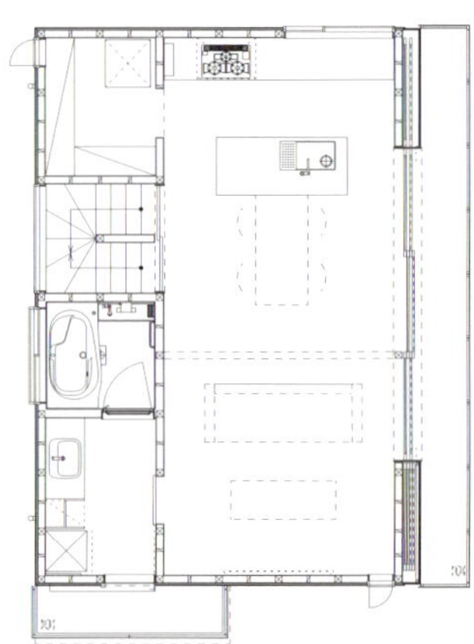

Second-floor plan

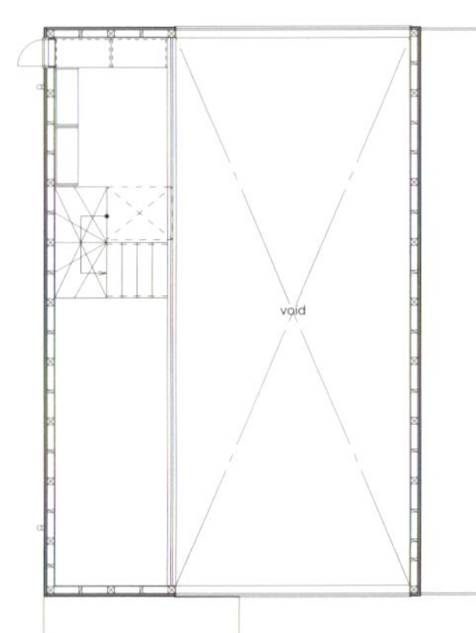

Loft plan

m Terrace

Design
Komada Takeshi, Komada Yuka
(Komada Architects Office)

Location
Tokyo

Completion
2017

Area
781 square feet (72.56 square meters)

Photography
Noboru Inoue

This project is located in a blind alley of a busy road in Tokyo. The architects decided to make a garden covering 40 percent of the lot.

Compared to the original wooden apartment building that seemed to block the line of sight, the project made a remarkably favorable landscape for the neighborhood. In the garden, the architects planted various trees, with Musashino forest vegetation in mind. Proceeding to the back, the garden connects with the neighbor's garden in the west, making a network of greenery. Each dwelling unit has a large entrance. The dwelling units form the nucleus of the living space, forming a place for various activities both inside and outside.

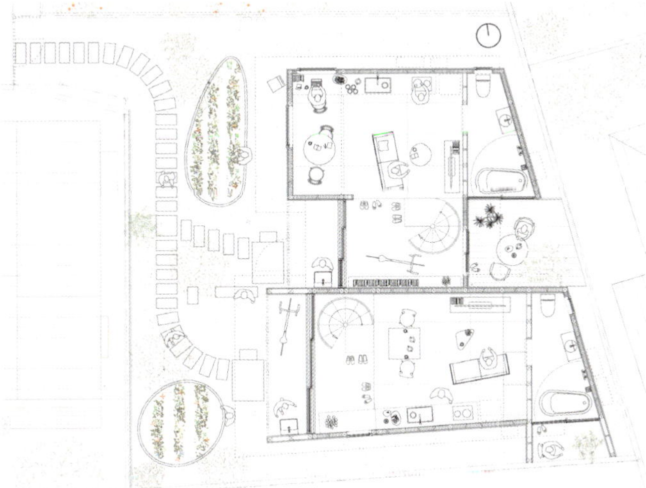

First-floor plan

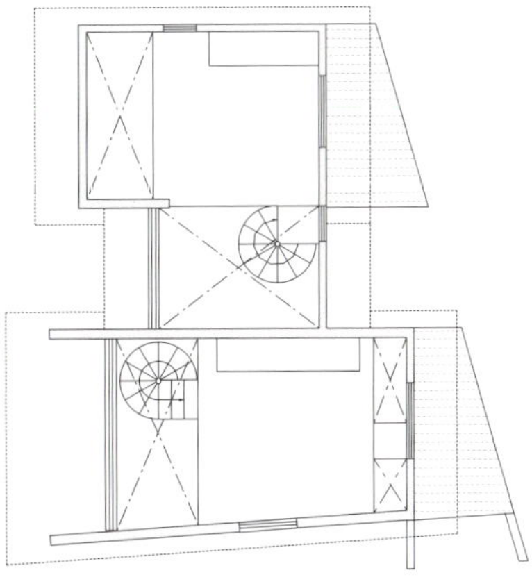

Second-floor plan

Section 1

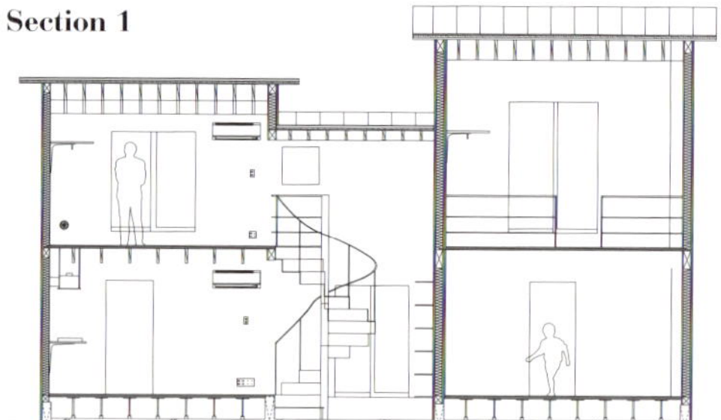

Section 2

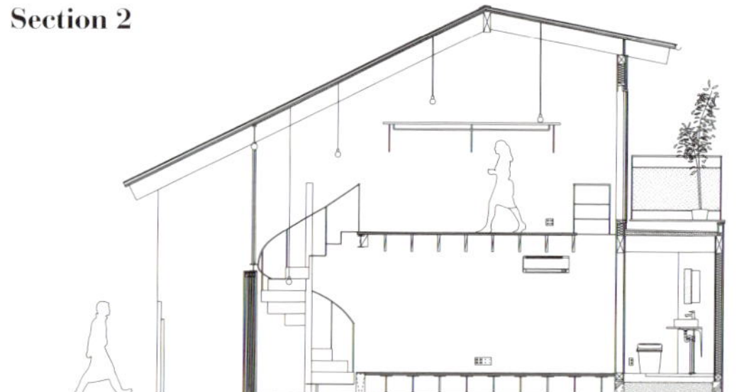

M10-house

Design
Masahiko Sato

Location
Kyushu

Completion
2016

Area
886.5 square feet (82.36 square meters)

Photography
Ikuma Satoshi

With a small court in its center, two structures with different height and material are neutralized by the L-shape eaves, creating a modern yet simple exterior appearance. Concrete objects with a varying heights were set up in the front exterior wall that utilized red cedar wood to deliver a deep impression of the building along with a sharp and warm atmosphere.

When one enters the entrance hall, a floating staircase will attract the eyes. Vegetation that is visible through the windows, together with indirect lighting that was installed under the stairs, enhances the overall ambience of the space. The indirect lighting on the second floor was designed to run along the ceiling down to the floor alongside the indirect lighting installed in the kitchen, the second-floor lighting creating a simple yet modern space. The living room is connected to a balcony, which has no opening on its side facing the main road, providing the residents with privacy.

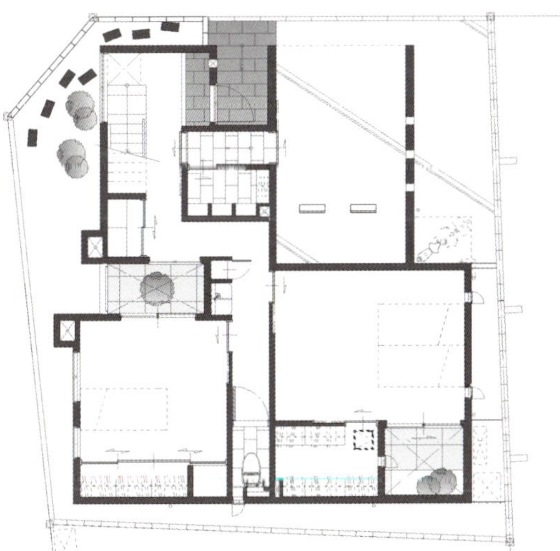

First-floor plan

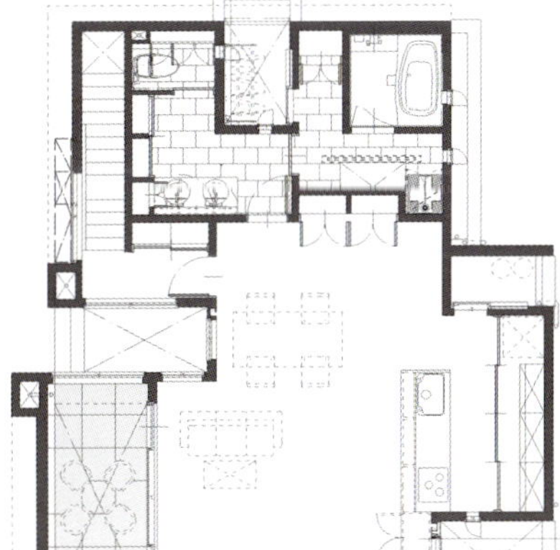

Second-floor plan

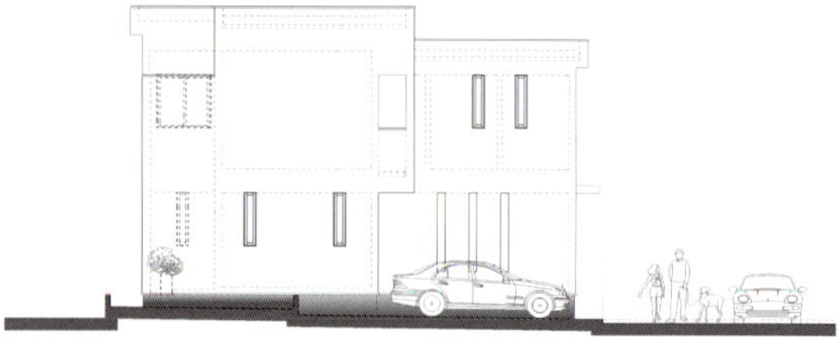

Elevation 1

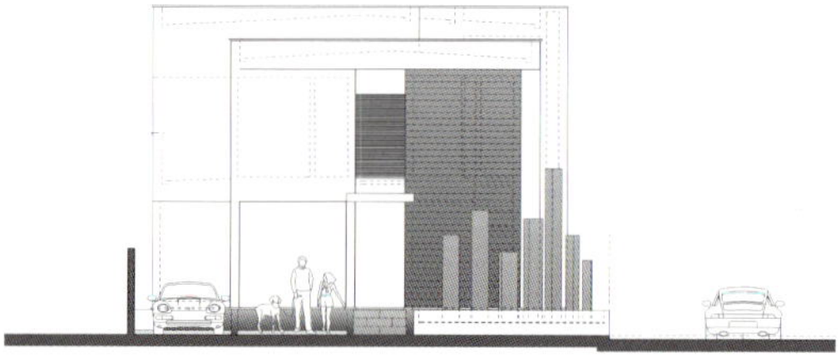

Elevation 2

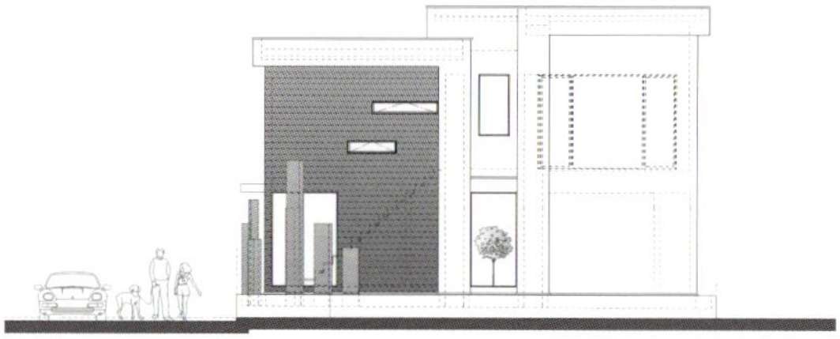

Elevation 3

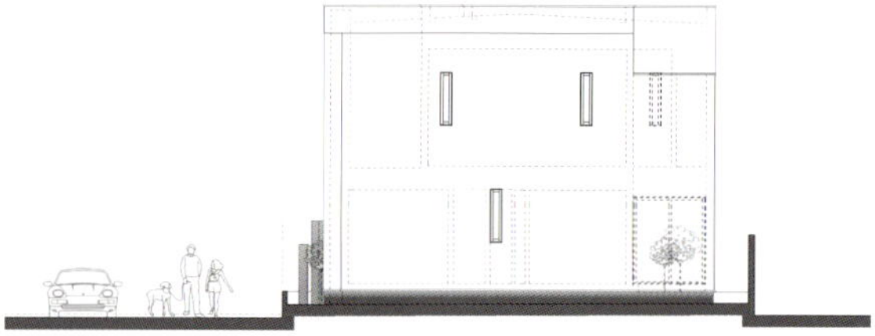

Elevation 4

Minimalist House

Design
Shinichi Ogawa & Associates

Location
Okinawa

Completion
2009

Area
1100.3 square feet (102.22 square meters)

Photography
Shinichi Ogawa & Associates, Shigeo Ogawa

The space composition is characterized by the division of the house into two areas by a piece of wall-like furniture. The first area is composed of a living room, dining room, and bedroom, connecting with the exterior courtyard in a linear arrangement. The other area is composed of a kitchen, bathroom, and study. All the spaces are combined together to create a lifestyle that minimizes the division of space as much as possible.

Given the amount of natural light available in Okinawa, the internal space was designed to maximize the direct sunlight coming into the house. The exterior wall was applied with a photocatalyst paint to facilitate maintenance.

The counter unit, which is made up of a kitchen, bathroom, and study is made of DuPont Corian. This house creates a space that encourages a minimalist and flexible lifestyle.

Plan

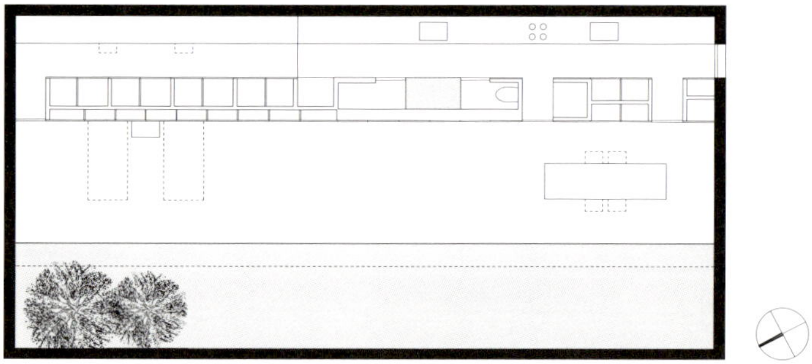

Motoyawata

Design
SNARK, OUVI

Location
Ichikawa

Completion
2017

Area
579.1 square feet (53.8 square meters)

Photography
Ippei Shinzawa

The project was surrounded by houses. In order to fill the room with wind and light, there was a colonnade in the center of the house. By connecting the entrance space to the whole house, the designers made it a zone with connections. The appearance responds to the urban landscape and the shape of the roof of the garage tower, gradually changing as the gradient changes. A new architectural space was created by taking over the shape of the house from ancient times and adapting the interior to modern life. The roof with steps brings depth and ventilation to the space, bringing light into the interior space. In a site with limited space, the arrangement of the bedroom, living, dining, and work areas were made to be as compact as possible.

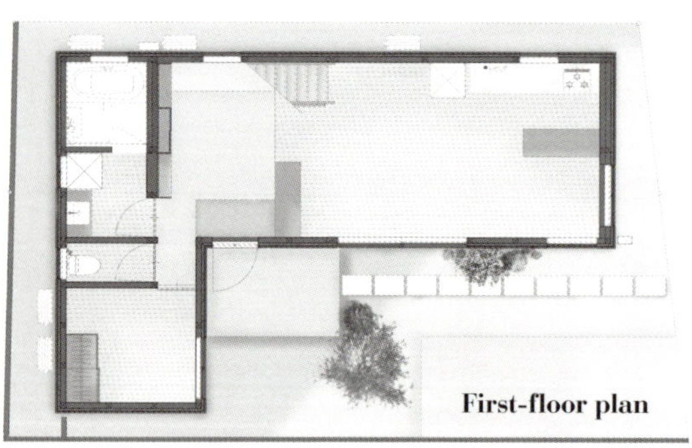

First-floor plan

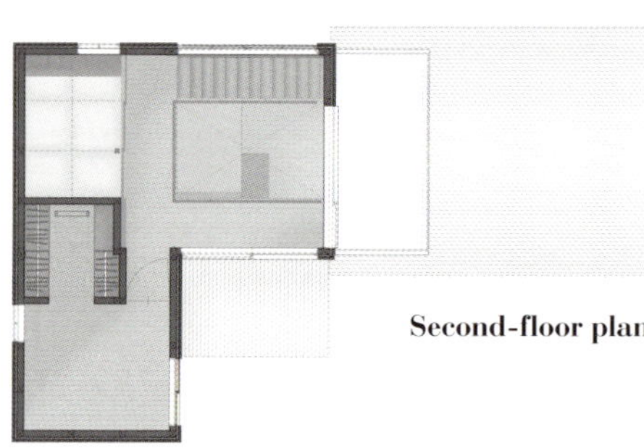

Second-floor plan

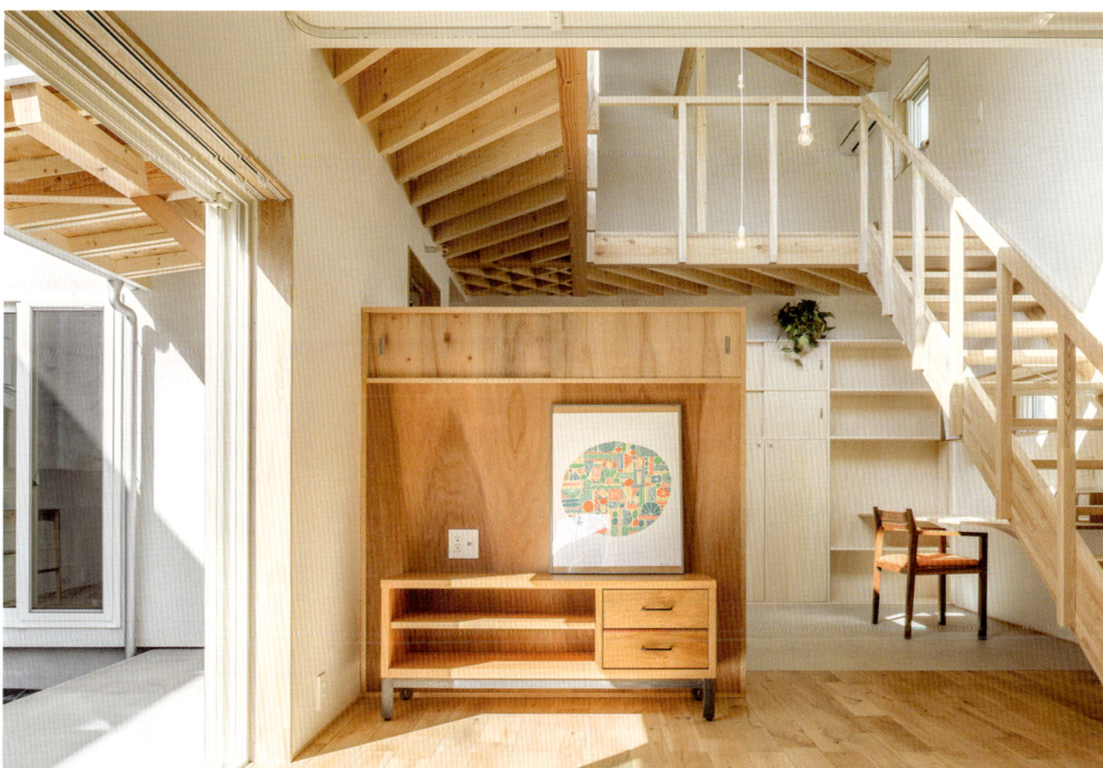

MoyaMoya

Design
Fumihiko Sano

Location
Tokyo

Completion
2014

Area
891.4 square feet (82.81 square meters)

Photography
Daisuke Shimokawa

The shape of the building plot is a huge square, sloping from north to south. Because of the sloped ground, the private space settled in the northern part commanded a fine view. An open ceiling studio is connected to a kitchen, allowing the client to have a big party whenever she desires. For when she ages in the future, her bedroom and the study were placed on the first floor. Guest rooms, a living room, and a Japanese-style room are on the second floor.

By creating a space that makes the border between the inside and the outside of the building vague, the inside as a consequence is difficult to see from the outside.

A special pattern is created because the stainless steel of the fence is doubled, making people feel as if they are inside even when they are outside. When the wind blows, the stainless steel fence shines and reflects a variety of patterns. The change of light over the course of the day not only creates other patterns on the fence, but also provides different impressions of the house.

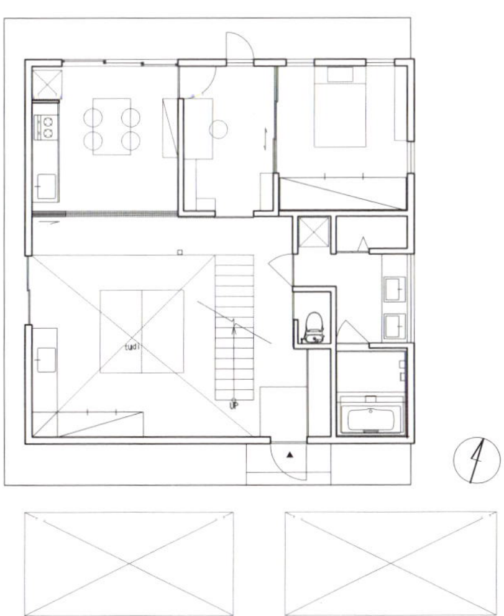

First-floor plan

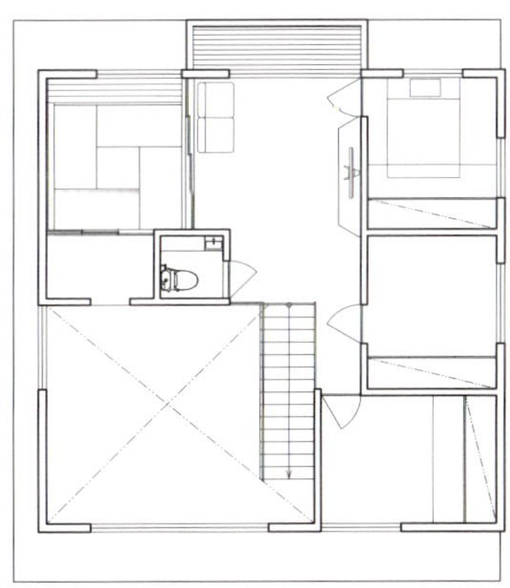

Second-floor plan

Nesting in the Circle

Design
Kazuhiko Kishimoto

Location
Zushi

Completion
2015

Area
1679.5 square feet (156.03 square meters)

Photography
Hiroshi Ueda

The house stands in the deep valley. Trees grow close together on both sides of the house, so the designer combined the living and dining areas on the second floor as one spacious room to take in the view, so people can enjoy it from the inside of the house. There are several spots drilled down cylindrically for the children and client couple to sit and relax, enjoy meals or watch movies; by doing so one spacious room shifts into smaller individual spaces. Each spot can be separated with curtains, which allows them to use the space according to their purposes.

First-floor plan

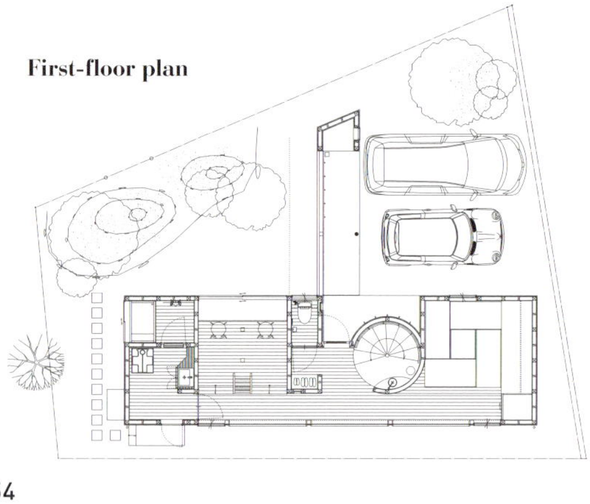

Second-floor plan

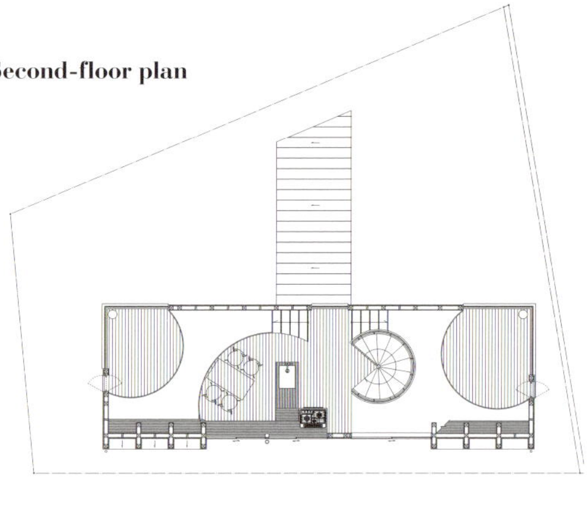

OKM 2014

Design
Artechnic

Location
Tokyo

Completion
2014

Area
2508 square feet (233 square meters)

Photography
Noboru Inoue

OKM is a four-story building designed for a private residence and apartment units located in Tokyo. The first and second floor provide a parking space and three apartment units, while the third and fourth floor hold the owner's residential space. There is a pocket park across the south side street. The building is intended to open up to this pocket park, at the same time, limiting visibility from the street level by creating three layers of hook-shaped exterior walls set on the façade.

These hook-shaped exterior walls also highlight the inner spacial structure. The upper volume of the building contains double volume space. The opening of this space is defined by these hook-shaped walls. There is a large opening located at the southeastern corner of the fourth floor to create a view of the skyscrapers in Shinjuku. The middle section of the hook-shaped walls works as balconies and handrails.

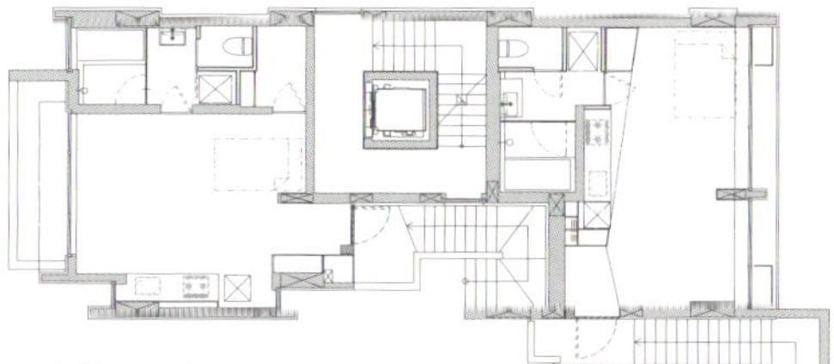

Second-floor plan

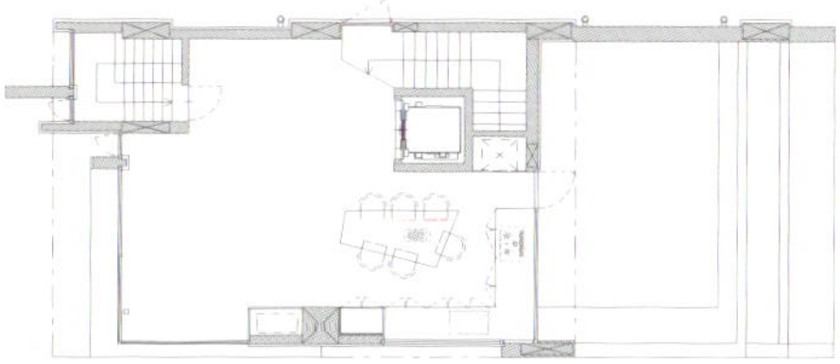

Fourth-floor plan

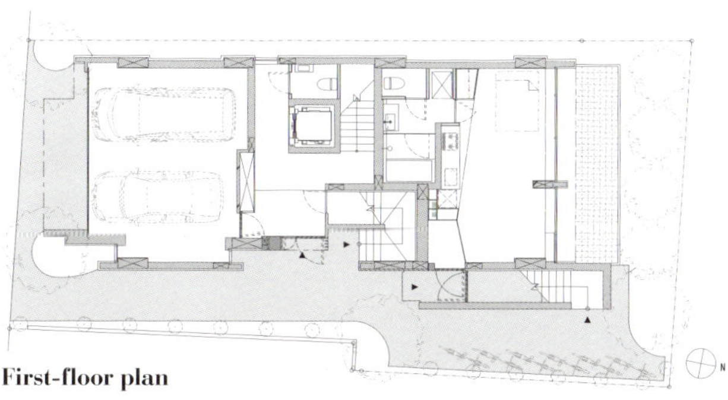

First-floor plan

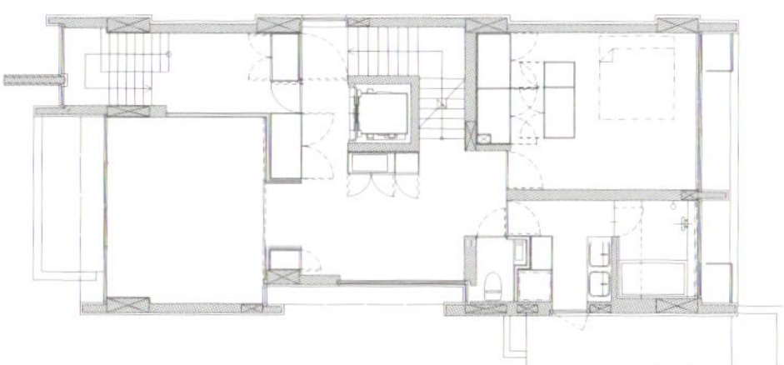

Third-floor plan

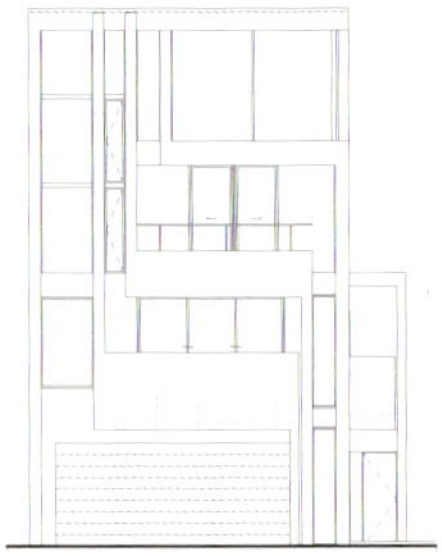

South elevation

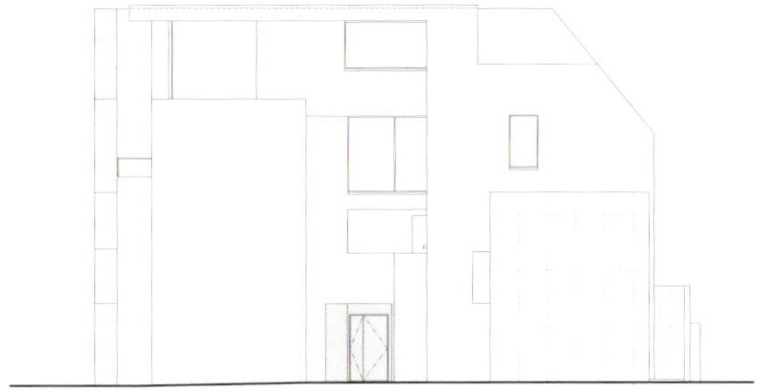

East elevation

North elevation

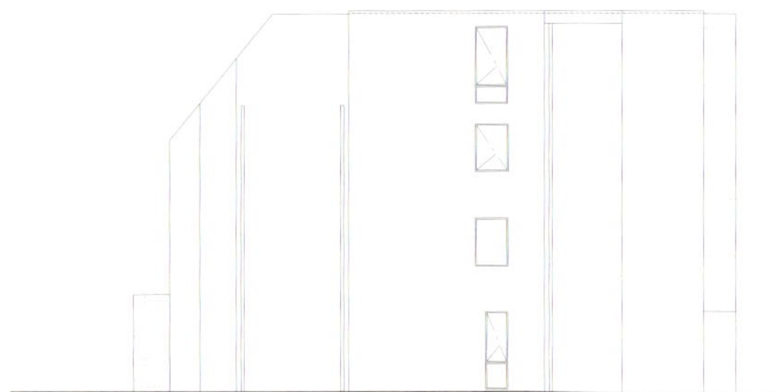

West elevation

Ouchi-36

Design
Jun Ishikawa, Kiyo Turu

Location
Tokyo

Completion
2016

Area
968.8 square feet (90 square meters)

Photography
Shigeo Ogawa

This is a house for three people—a father and two daughters. The appearance is a combination of two triangular roofs, white walls and the black roof. The owner's request was to be able to park his Austin Rover Mini on the premises as well as make a private room for his two daughters and a room for himself. The designer trimmed the shape of the building into a rectangle and squeezed out space for parking. The designer arranged a living room on the second floor that is well lit with natural light and placed the private rooms for the two daughters on the first floor. The interior used a white wall and a black wall. The white wall has the function of reflecting light, making the interior bright. Conversely, the black wall absorbs light.

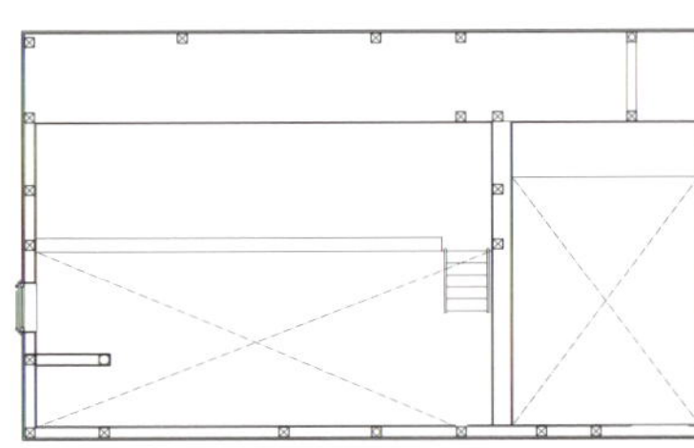

Third-floor plan

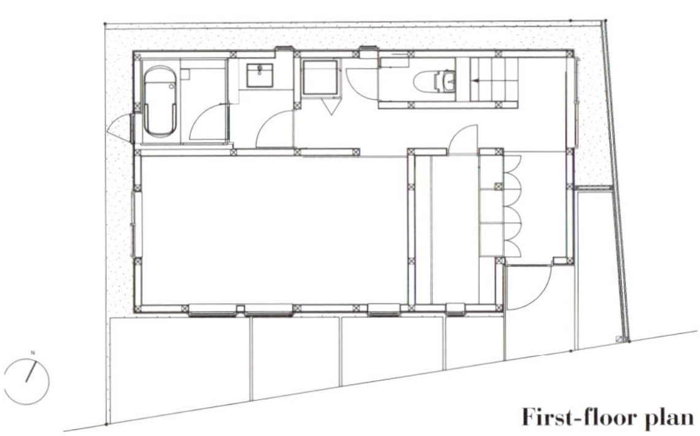

First-floor plan

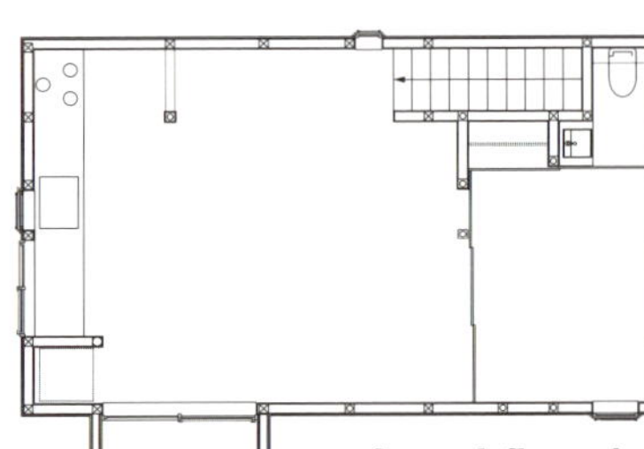

Second-floor plan

Ouchi-37

Design
Jun Ishikawa, Naoko Ishikawa

Location
Tokyo

Completion
2016

Area
925.7 square feet (86 square meters)

Photography
Hiroshi Ueda

This house's design was influenced by origami, experimenting with the design by folding the façade. The ridge line of the diagonal roof and the balcony are designed to look like a single folding plane, as if it was all made of paper.

In front of the premises, there is a large manor. Also, in considering the placement of windows, the designer built a wall for privacy. A master bedroom and a children's room are on the first floor, while a living room and atelier are arranged on the second floor. The bathroom was placed in the extra space of the second floor.

The interior was finished in white tones, allowing enjoyment of the sunlight as it changes in color throughout the day. In the same way, the appearance was also based on white finish, with some black painted wooden accents. Walls with black wood boards were also used to give the building a Japanese style.

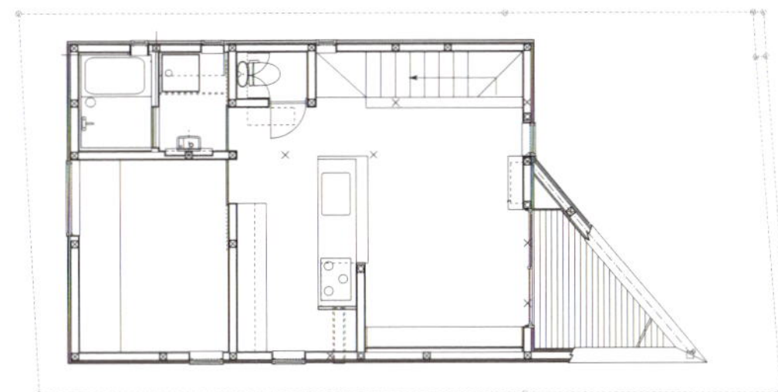

Second-floor plan

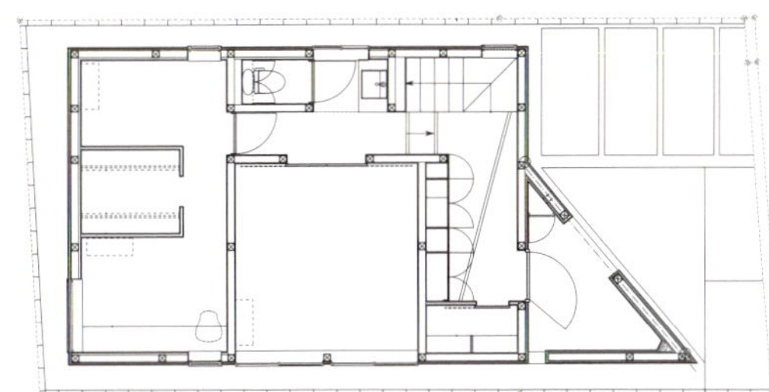

First-floor plan

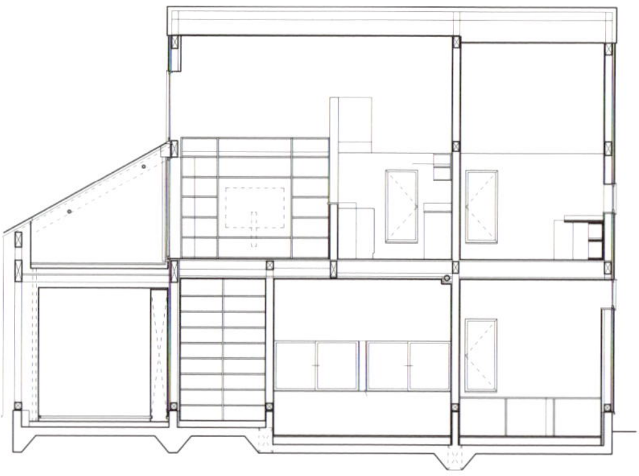

Section 1

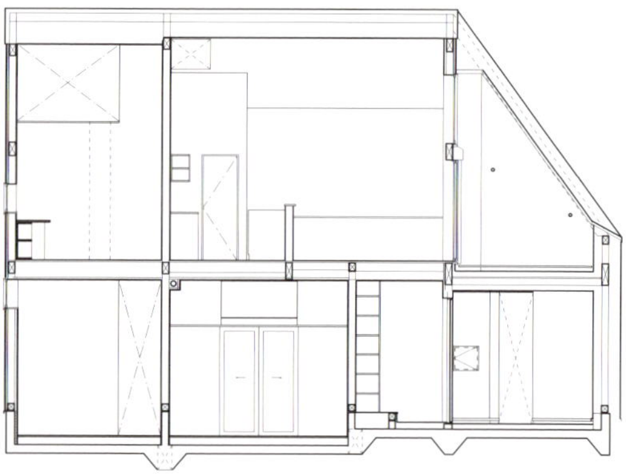

Section 2

Patio

Design
Satoshi Kurosaki
(APOLLO Architects & Associates)

Location
Kawasaki, Kanagawa

Completion
2015

Area
721.3 square feet (67.01 square meters)

Photography
Masao Nishikawa

The contrast between the exterior walls covered with strips of red cedar in dark brown color and the white volume sticking out on the second floor gives off a striking impression of the building.

In contrast to the stoic exterior with confined expression, an airy patio space filled with natural light rests inside as the core of the interior spaces. This patio space enables easy and casual access between the Japanese-style room with tatami mat adjacent to the entrance and the main bedroom situated across the patio.

Built-in furniture was installed next to the living area for storing books and CDs, while large sliding doors were installed for uniting this area with the exterior living area. The dining and kitchen area is situated on a raised floor, allowing gradual separation of the dining and kitchen area from the living area.

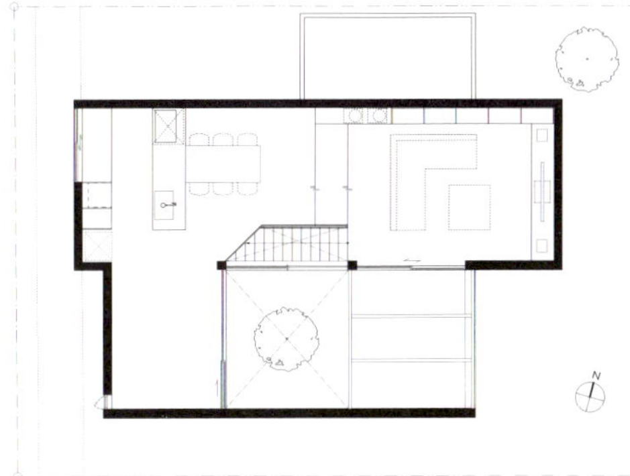

Second-floor plan

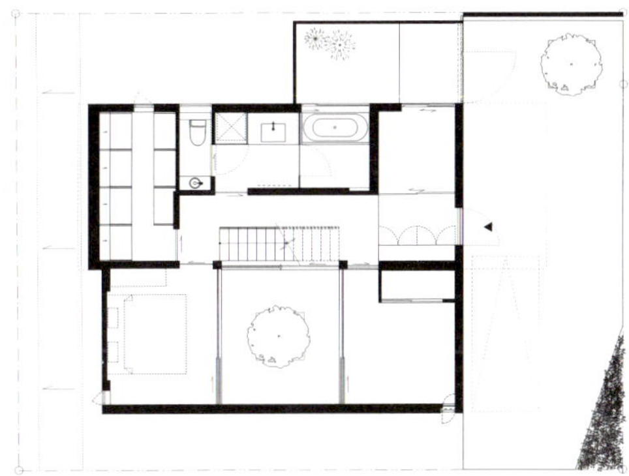

First-floor plan

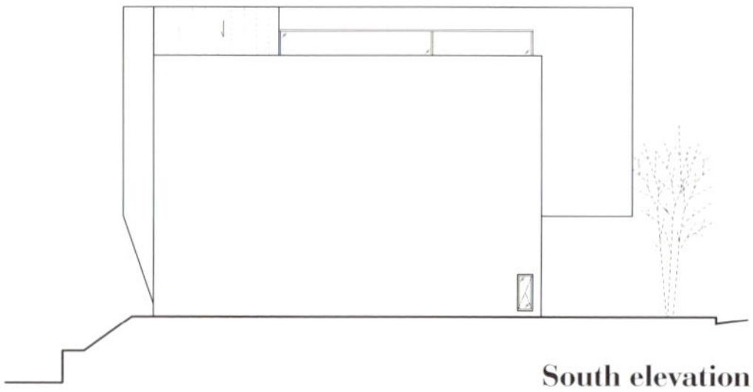

South elevation

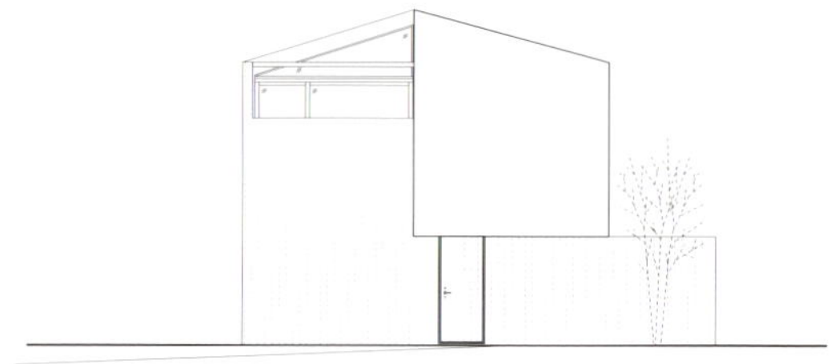

East elevation

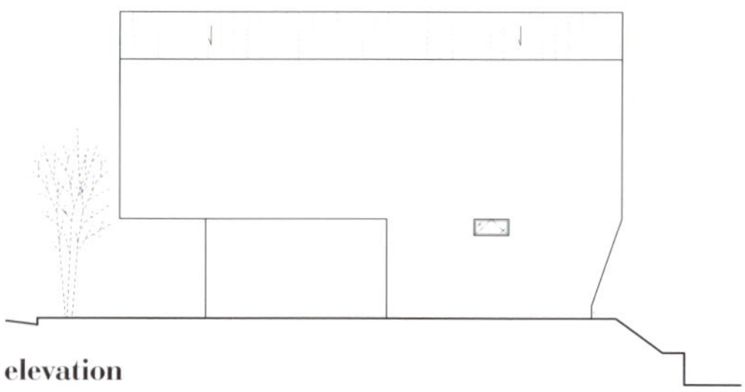

North elevation

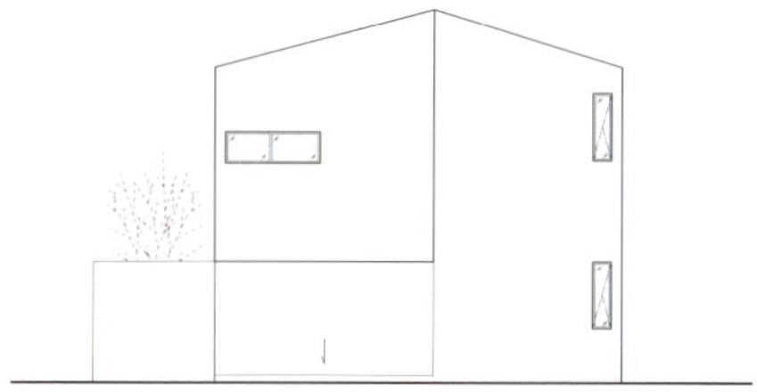

West elevation

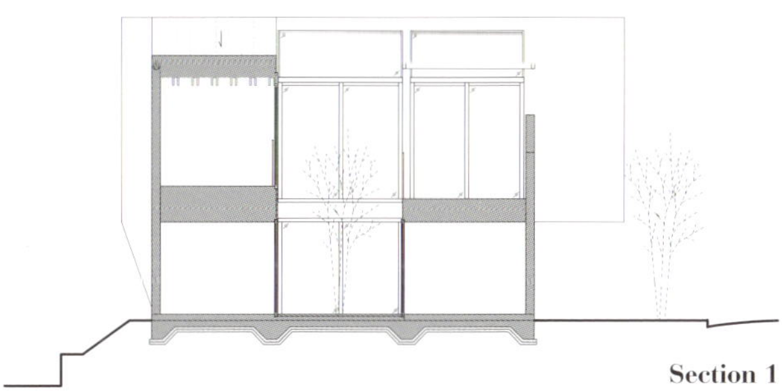

Section 1

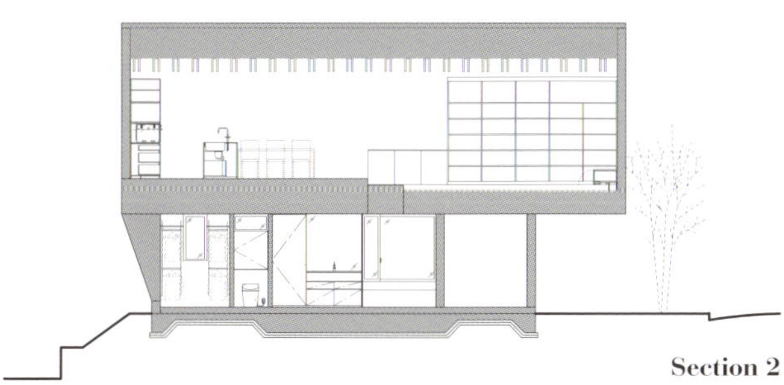

Section 2

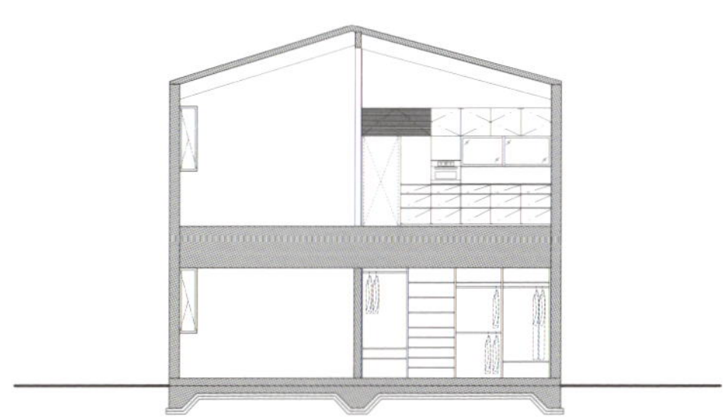

Section 3

Pergola

Design
Satoshi Kurosaki
(APOLLO Architects & Associates)

Location
Kawaguchi, Saitama

Completion
2014

Area
552.5 square feet (51.33 square meters)

Photography
Masao Nishikawa

The house has a simple L-shaped plan, built around a covered courtyard in the center, decreasing construction costs. The covered courtyard, also used as an entrance, serves as an intermediate space between the inside and outside.

The main bedroom, located next to the entrance on the first floor, is a small private room with a sense of calmness. On the other hand, the children's room is an open space located next to the courtyard. Skeleton stairs, which can also be appreciated as an art piece, are located in front of the main entrance, leading to the second floor. The second floor is comprised of an open space without partitions. The space is defined by a sequence of beautifully exposed wood ceiling rafters. The wood rafters extend to outside and constitute a pergola above the entrance courtyard, integrating the interior and exterior spaces.

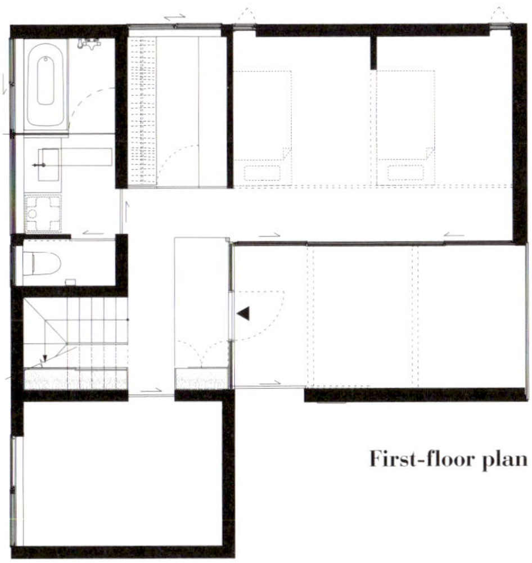

First-floor plan

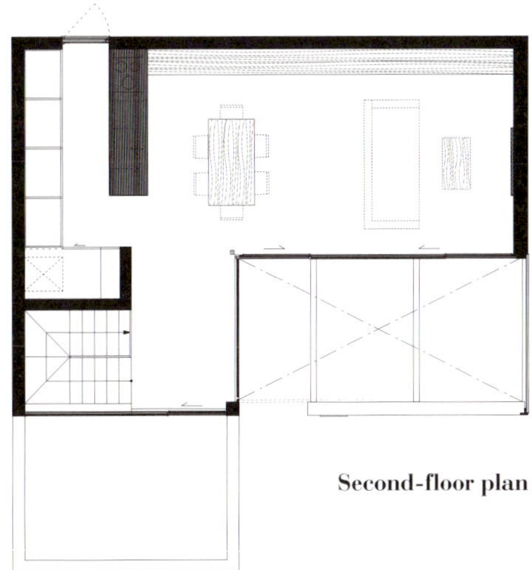

Second-floor plan

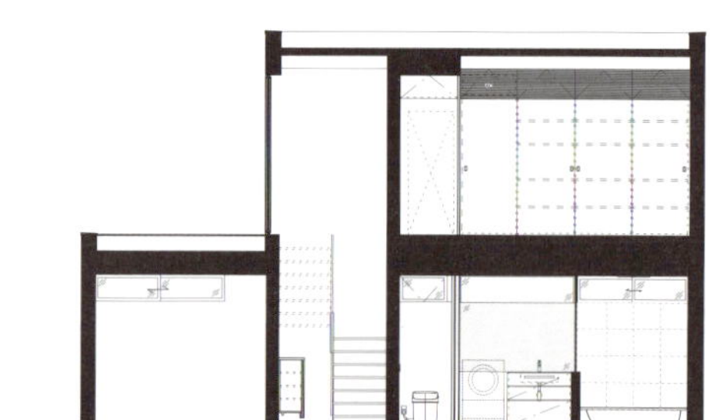

Section 1

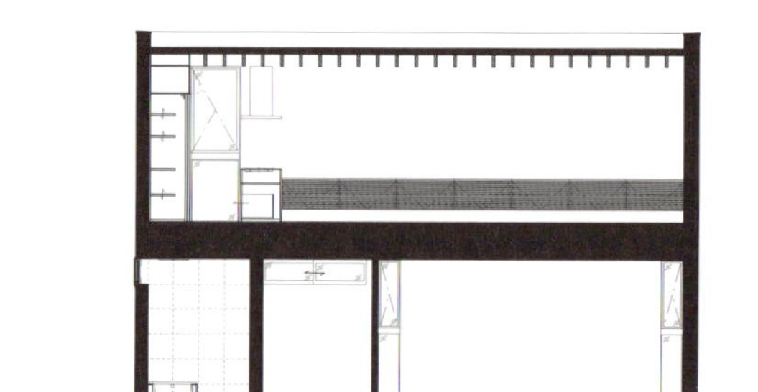

Section 2

Platform

Design
Takanobu Kishimoto

Location
Takasago, Hyogo

Completion
2014

Area
934 square feet (86.77 square meters)

Photography
Eiji Tomita

When making site surveys, designers found a train near the site, which has been there since the client was young. The train used to be open to the public and has now become a rest area for people. Through pursuing local news bulletins, the designers understood the role the train had in contributing to the area's local heritage. The designers preserved the train and used it to enhance the project, rather than completely dismantling it. Therefore, the house beside the train has been built like a platform. To adjust the ground level, the designers used a concrete foundation to create the platform as a cantilevered siding, which can also be used as a place for firewood. The north side of the house facing the train has a large opening to get enough sunlight. The platform seems to be far away from daily life, but it serves as a new living space that is closely connected with the community.

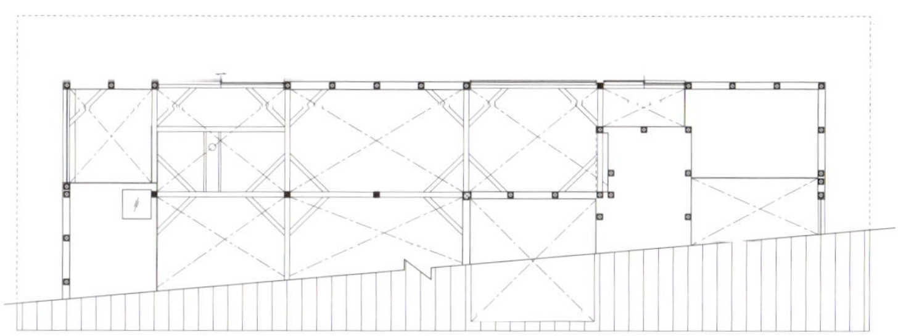

Loft plan

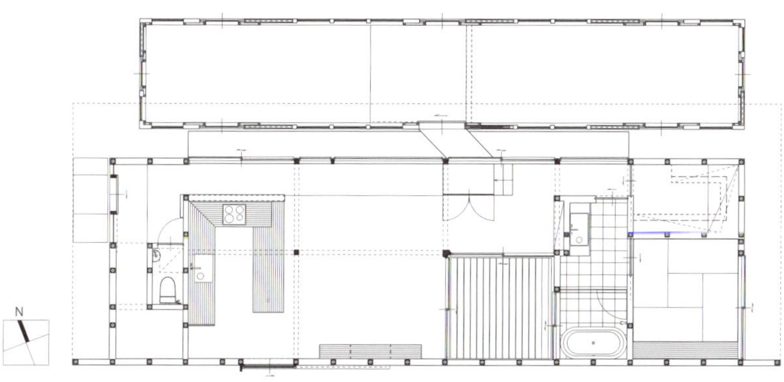

First-floor plan

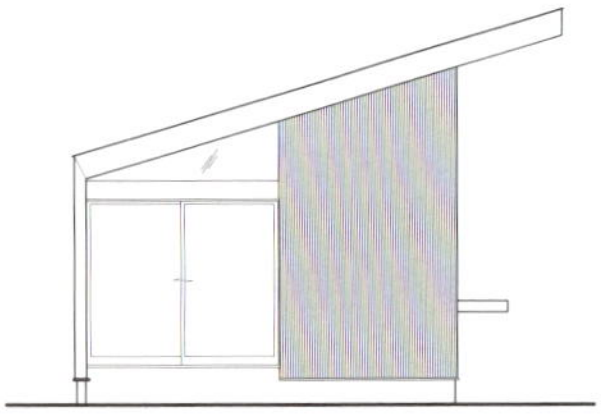

East elevation

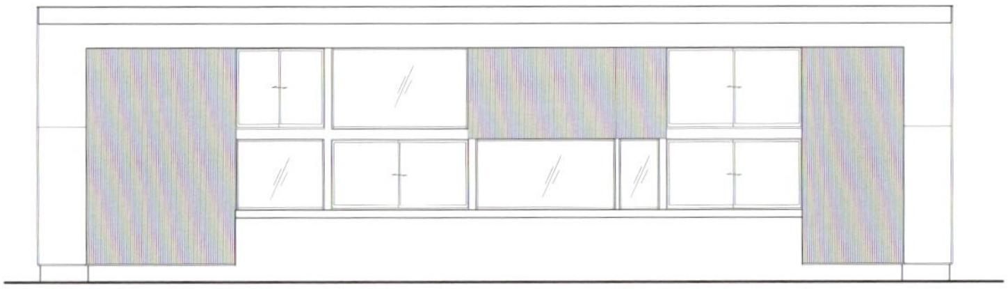

North elevation

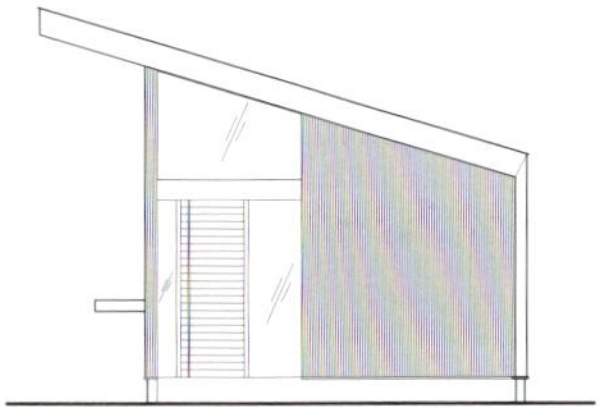

West elevation

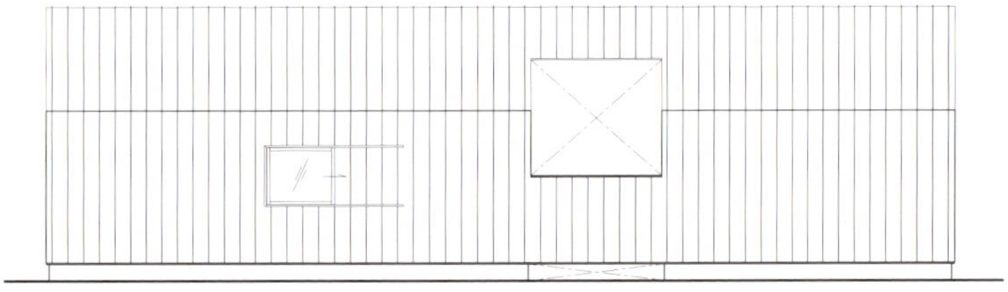

South elevation

Plug

Design
studio LOOP

Location
Gunma

Completion
2015

Area
1241.2 square feet (115.31 square meters)

Photography
Kai Nakamura

Plug is a house located in Gunma, Japan. This is a project for a husband, wife, and their son. Located in the north is a road, to the east is a neighboring house, to the west and the south are fields. The fields offer a fascinating view. The designers proposed a plan that cut out three corners excluding the southeast. The purpose was to decrease costs by decreasing the floor area, but the designers also thought that the design would create a dramatic change in view. The entrance has a large concrete floor, and a full-height window to illuminate the space and a staircase. The open concept living, dining, and kitchen area has a window slightly below eye level, providing a view of the greenery outside. On the southern end, the ribbon windows merge into one large window. Beyond that, there is a wooden deck where the ceiling of the living room sticks out, and the deck juts out to the field. At the east end of the deck, it raises up to the roof to add privacy to the bathroom. On the second floor, there is a large terrace that is surrounded by three bed rooms.

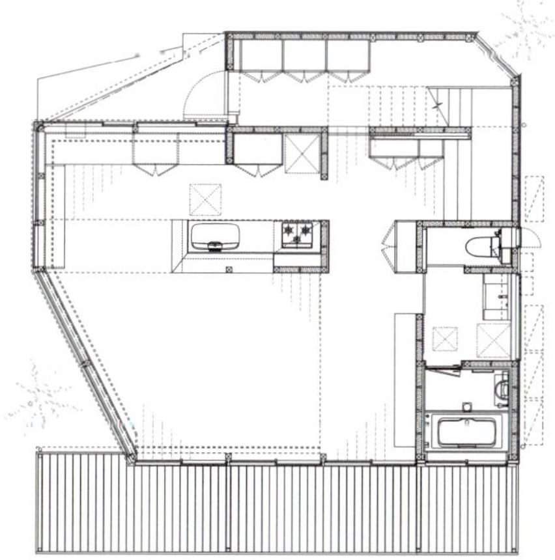

First-floor plan

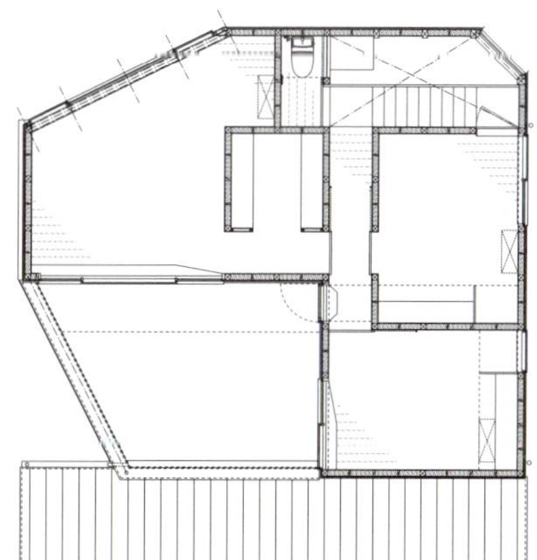

Second-floor plan

JUDGE NOT.
BEFORE YOU
JUDGE
YOURSELF.

Roof & Shelter

Design
Kazuhiko Kishimoto

Location
Kamakura

Completion
2015

Area
851.7 square feet (79.13 square meters)

Photography
Hiroshi Ueda

This house is located in a triangle-shaped site that faces a beautiful pedestrian path. On fine days, there are many people taking a walk on the path as a hiking trail. Given this risk of passers-by looking in, the designer set the floor higher than usual and connected each floor with stairs so people outside cannot look inside. The large stairway in the living room was planned to function as a place where the family can sit and get comfortable any time they wish. On the other hand, unlike the second floor with bright open space, the first floor was designed as an alcove with plenty of shade.

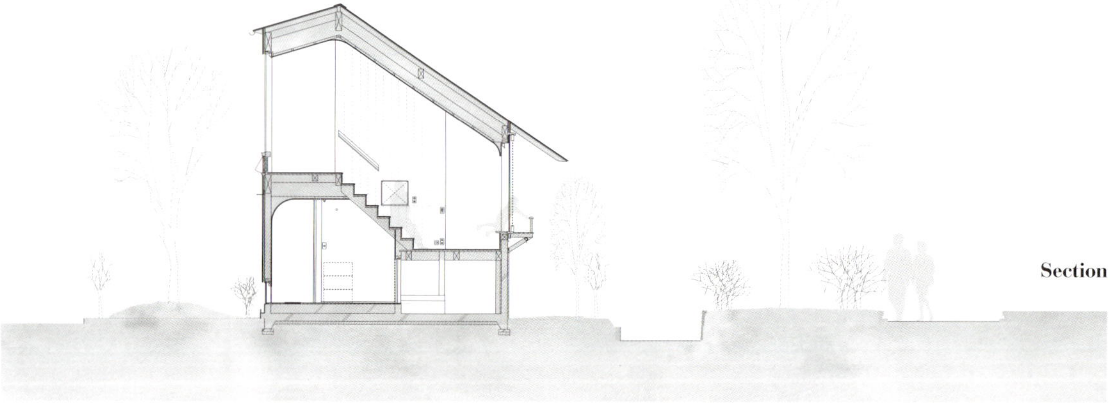

Section

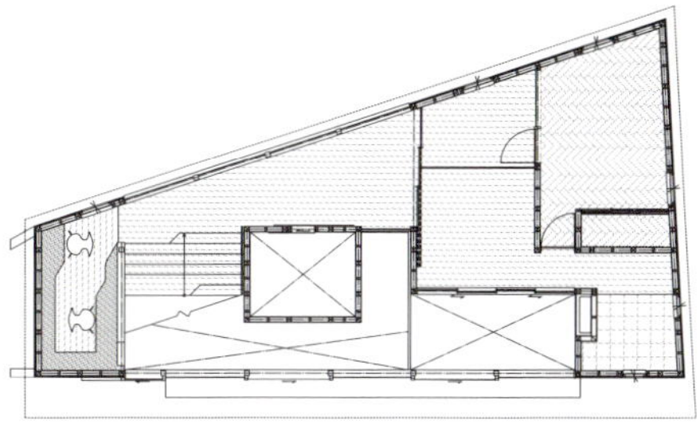

Second-floor plan

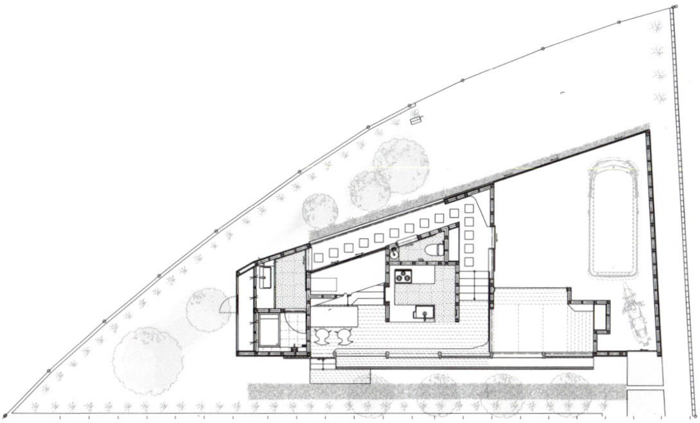

First-floor plan

SANKAKU

Design
Spatial Design Studio

Location
Yamanashi

Completion
2016

Area
1471.1 square feet (136.67 square meters)

Photography
Kaoru Yamada

SANKAKU, 'triangle' in Japanese, is a mountain house atop 4921-foot (1500-meter) highlands in Yatsugatake. The design was aimed to be in harmony with its surroundings in its simplicity and efficiency. This project inclines to the south, with a 18-foot (5.5-meter) elevation difference overall. By exploiting this difference, the location of the two buildings was carefully placed to protect the privacy of residents and to frame views of the surrounding mountains.

The triangular roof is made of folded planks, which are made of laminated pine wood. These wood planks are both structural and serve as a finish. The bigger building houses the main facilities, including a kitchen and full bathroom. The smaller one, having only a commode instead of a full bathroom, is used as a study room or a guest room. Each building is essentially one room, with the addition of doors for bathrooms. However, two separate buildings enable a variety of uses.

The simple shape of SANKAKU allows people to enjoy each other's company while being surrounded by rugged and abundant nature.

Plan

Section

Shift House

Design
KINO architects (Masahiro Kinoshita)

Location
Tokyo

Completion
2015

Area
464.6 square feet (43.16 square meters)

Photography
Kai Nakamura

The shifted shape creates a variety of spaces inside and outside of the house, forming a blank space that can be shifted to match the family's changing needs.

The house's big gabled roof follows an oblique line. It created a small gap around the building by dividing the house into four sections and shifting them to the left and right. Instead of direct contact between the inside and the outside by a wall or a window, the project connects with the city at a reasonable distance through the space created around the building. The interior space is gently segmented by shifting. The interior space is felt much larger than it actually is. Additionally, it was possible to secure sufficient daylighting and ventilation from a small window by placing the window on the wall where the gap is.

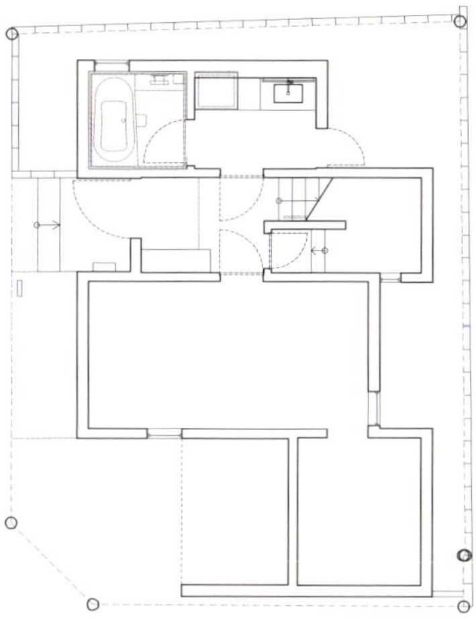

First-floor plan

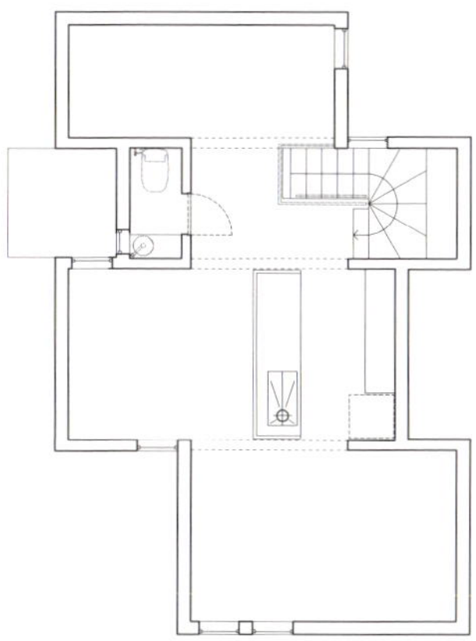

Second-floor plan

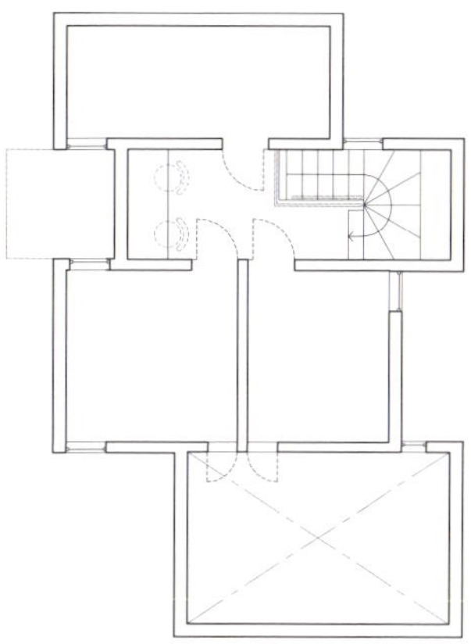

Loft plan (forward planning)

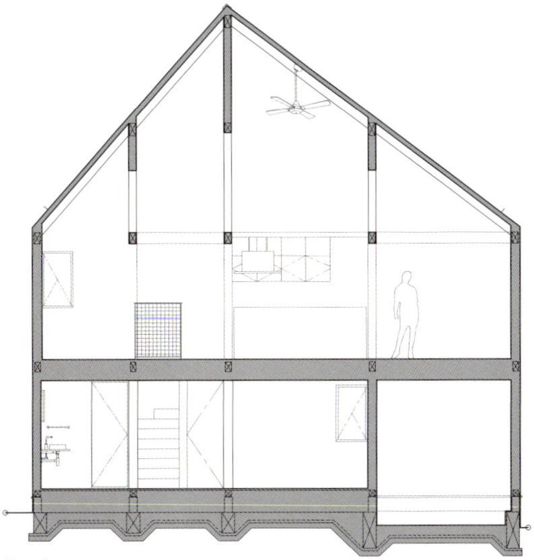

Section

Solid Cedar House

Design
Shigeru Ban Architects

Location
Hokuto, Yamanashi

Completion
2015

Area
1556.5 square feet (144.6 square meters)

Photography
Hiroyuki Hirai

This project was developed as an extension of some on-going works. In the same way that Mies Van der Rohe used concrete and brick as partition walls in order to create a sequence of connecting interior space with exterior landscape, the solid cedar walls cut out various views within the different spaces that are located in this work. The walls not only frame the views, but also function to conceal neighboring houses and roads.

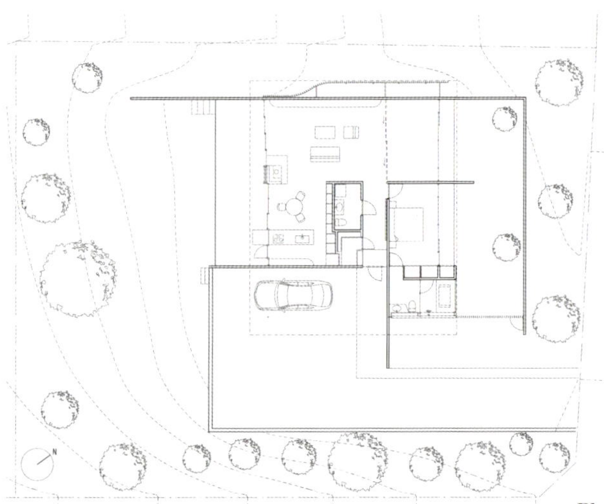

Plan

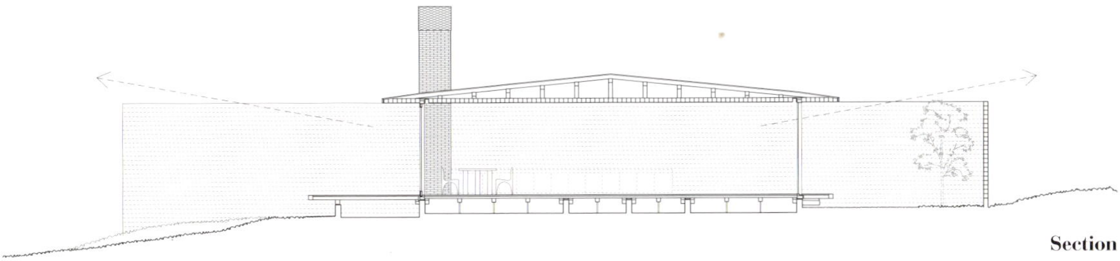

Section

SUBAKO

Design
Takuya Tsuchida, Kano Hirano

Location
Ota Ward

Completion
2016

Area
1387.9 square feet (128.94 square meters)

Photography
Ryoma Suzuki

While the east and the west sides are closed because of the neighboring houses, the designers opened up the south and north sides. They left the south side wide-open to increase natural light and did the same for the north side to add visibility to the surrounding scenery. The designers built a terrace surrounded by walls outside of the opening, which both ensures privacy and blocks wind from the northwest. The house has two intermediate floors, giving sufficient spaces for the owner to store a number of items for work and hobby.

Due to the relationship between the orientations and each room, the whole house cannot be symmetrical. However, as the designer treated the surrounding environment symmetrically, the shape of the house itself feels symmetrical. While each room plays a different role, no single room seems prioritized over others. The interior is like a bird's nest surrounded by greenery.

Loft plan

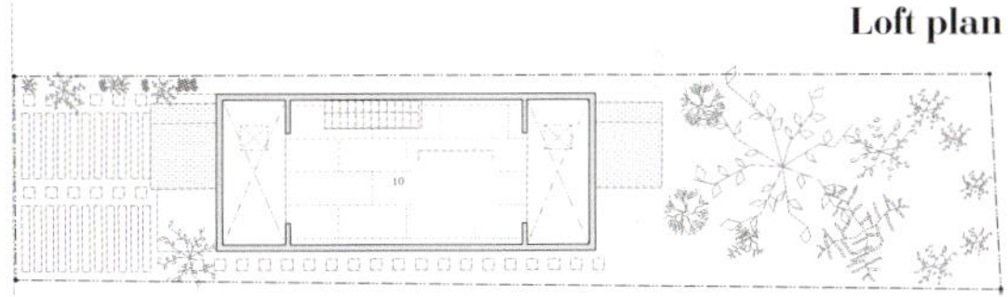

Second-floor plan

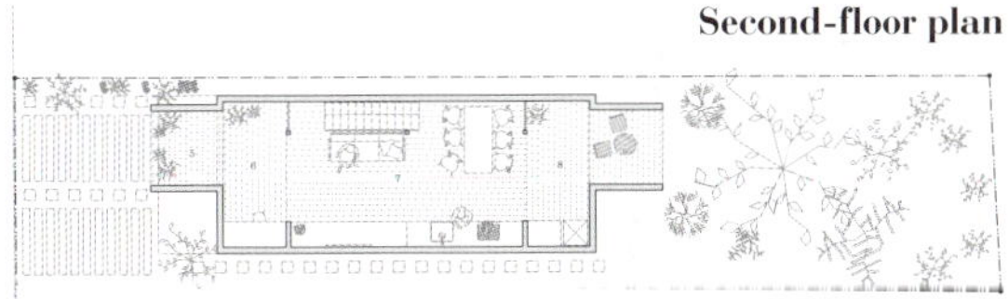

Intermediate-floor plan

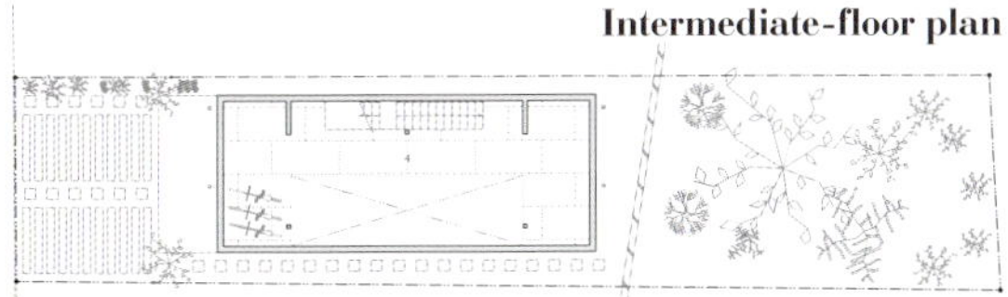

First-floor plan

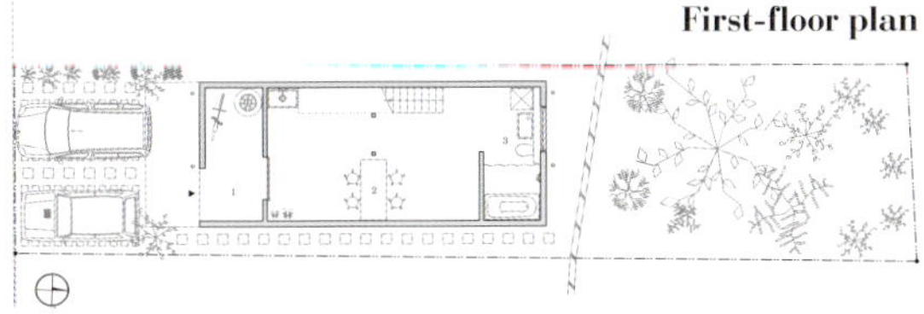

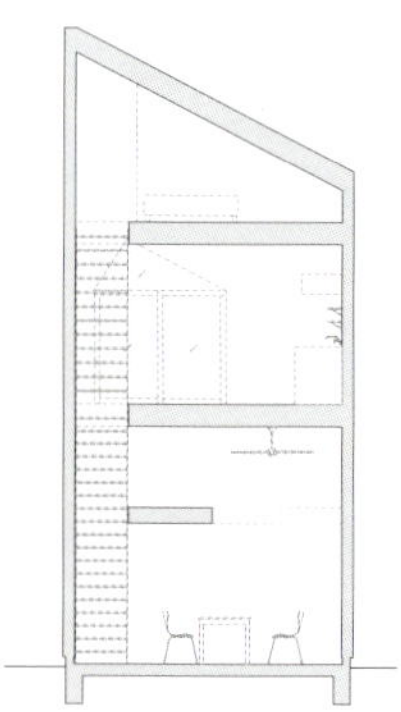

Section 1

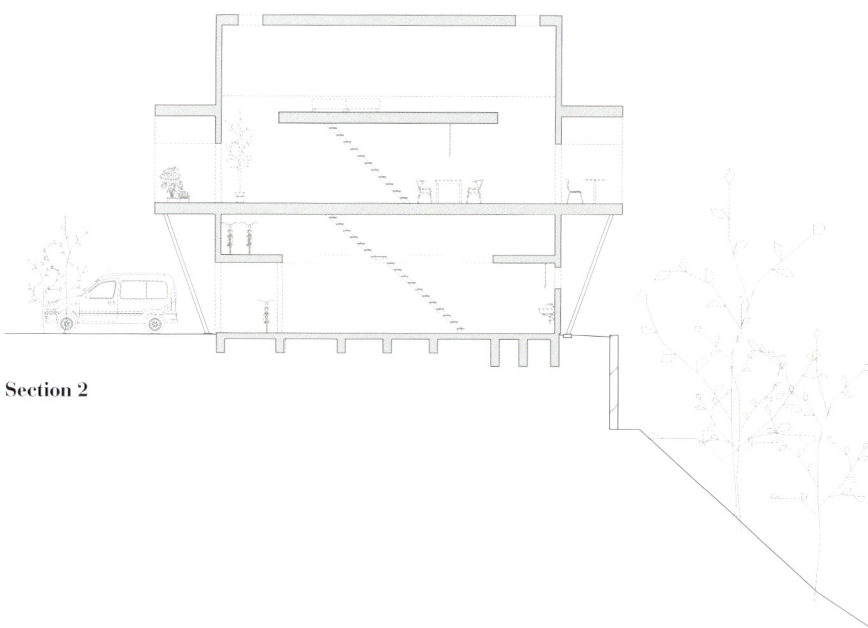

Section 2

MAD&VIN

SUKIMA

Design
Takuya Tsuchida, Kano Hirano

Location
Hiratsuka

Completion
2015

Area
1247.3 square feet (115.88 square meters)

Photography
Shunichi Koyama

The house is for a couple and their two children amid a row of new houses in a residential area in Hiratsuka. The building's boundaries were resized so that the garden and parking space can be generated on the remaining space. Clearance space was provided even inside. Clearance space was formed between two wooden boxes, creating a living room. Such a space can even transition into other sections. By opening the top and bottom of the wooden boxes, a dining area and bedroom are created. The clearance space without the wooden boxes would be a two-story atrium with a rich volume. In other words, linked with each other, the clearance spaces are developed into spontaneous spaces. The entire building is kept very compact. The perception of the width and the height changes depending on where one stays in the house, and it makes the house feel wider and larger than the actual area.

First-floor plan

Second-floor plan

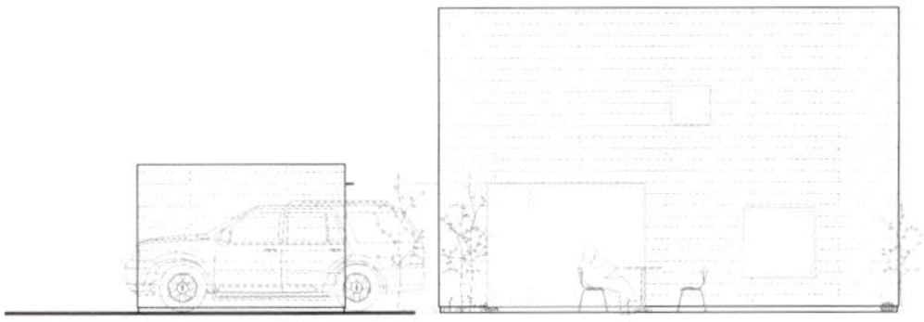

South elevation

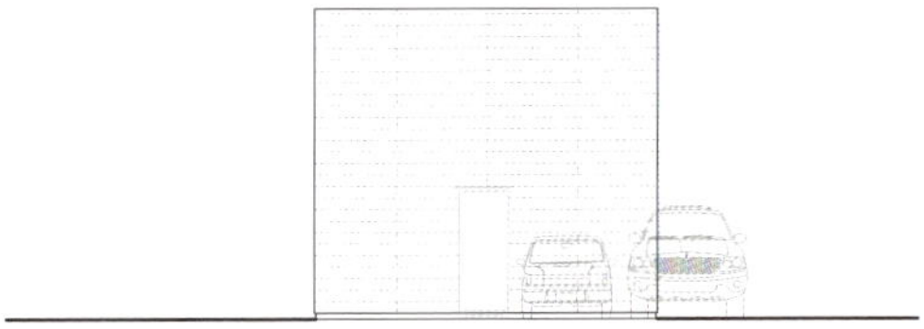

East elevation

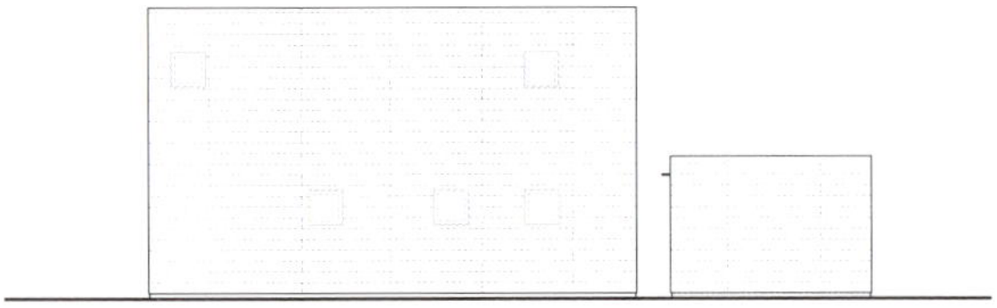

North elevation

West elevation

Sunomata

Design
Keitaro Muto

Location
Gifu

Completion
2014

Area
2002.1 square feet (186 square meters)

Photography
Teruaki Yoshiike

The building has been designed as a series of layers that step down towards the rice fields to the west. This played an important role on how the internal spaces were organized. For the reconstruction of the existing Japanese garden, the big stones were left in the same positions, and small stones were randomly decorated across the site. The layered spaces interact with the gardens to create a parallel relationship between the gardens and the house.

The parent's living room, entrance, bathroom, study, and lounge are lined up sequentially inside the house. Each of the internal spaces has a different relationship to the Japanese garden, whether this is visual or physical.

Second-floor plan

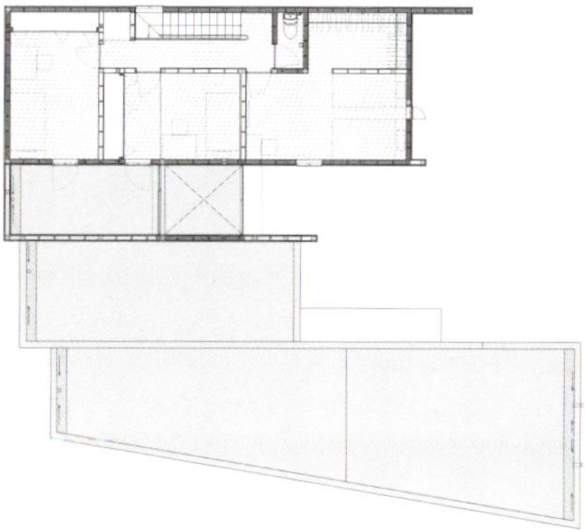

First-floor plan

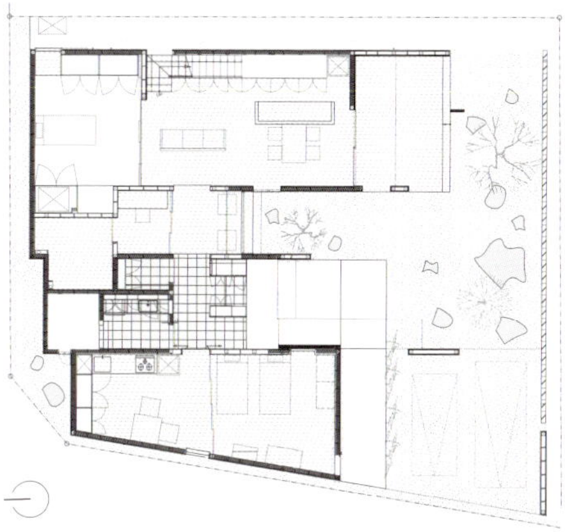

North elevation

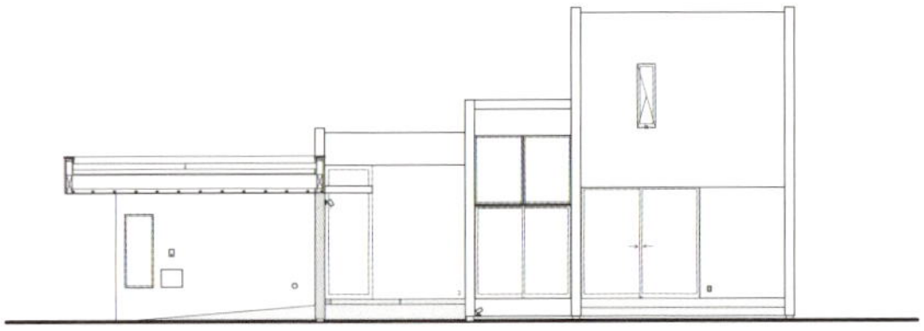

South elevation

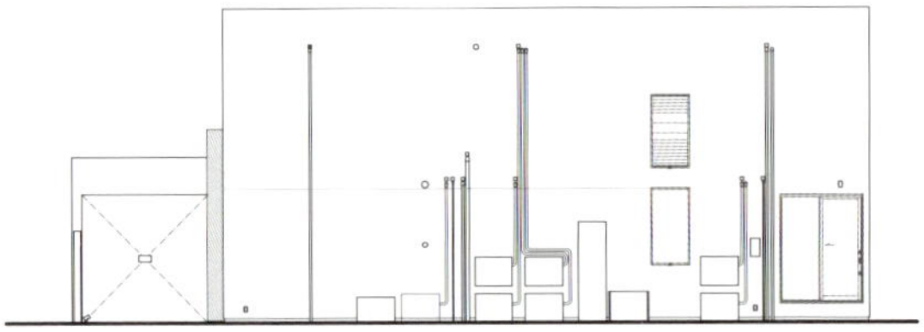

East elevation

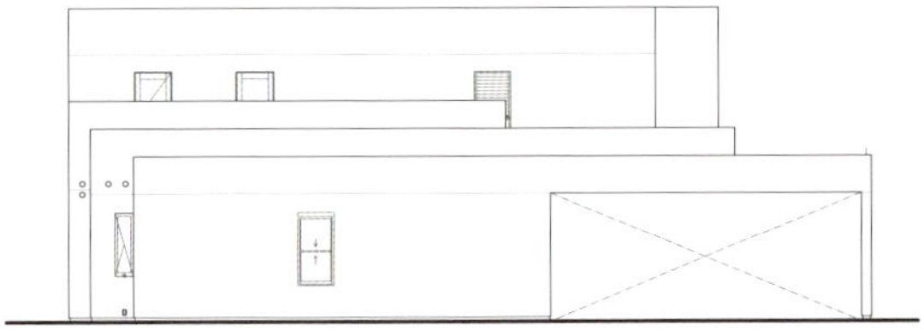

West elevation

Surrounded House

Design
Masahiro Miyake (y+M design office)

Location
Osaka

Completion
2016

Area
1443.3 square feet (134.09 square meters)

Photography
Yohei Sasakura

The site is located in a residential area with relatively large compartment in Hirakata, Osaka. There are many houses with sloping roofs, as well as the concrete block fences on the site boundary line. The architects thought the new house built in such a residential area should blend into the surroundings.

The client is a family with five members including a couple and three children, and they hope to have a healthy lifestyle in a comfortable living environment, not depending on the air conditioner as much as possible.

Since the site is crowded, taking into consideration daylighting and ventilation, the house was made into the so-called courtyard type to ensure privacy. Furthermore, by adjusting the height, gradient, and direction of the gable roof that has been divided into several parts, it ensures daylighting, humidity, and privacy. Because only several necessary load-bearing walls were arranged to support those gable roofs, the concrete block fence surrounds the space so as to sew the layout while penetrating inside and outside respectively. The wall of the concrete block is functioned as site boundary line, partition wall, blindfold wall, structural reinforcement, as well as keeping out the noise of the parking lot in the northern side.

Each room has a small garden surrounded by the concrete block walls, ensuring ventilation to pass through the courtyard terrace, creating brightness and liberating feeling, as well as securing privacy.

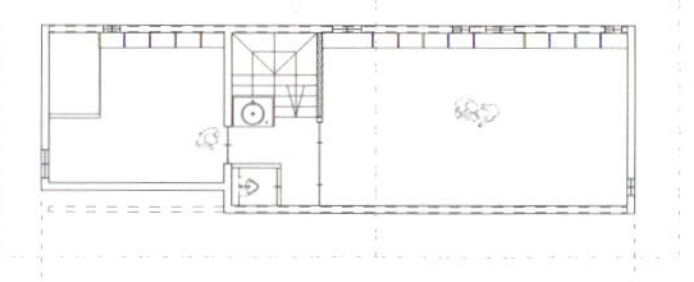

Second-floor plan

First-floor plan

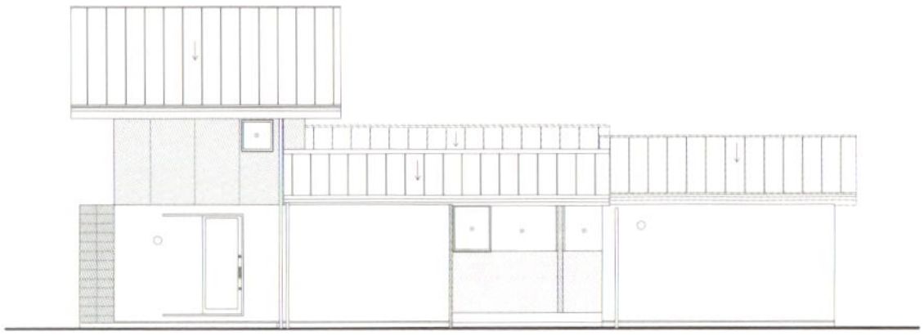

South elevation

East elevation

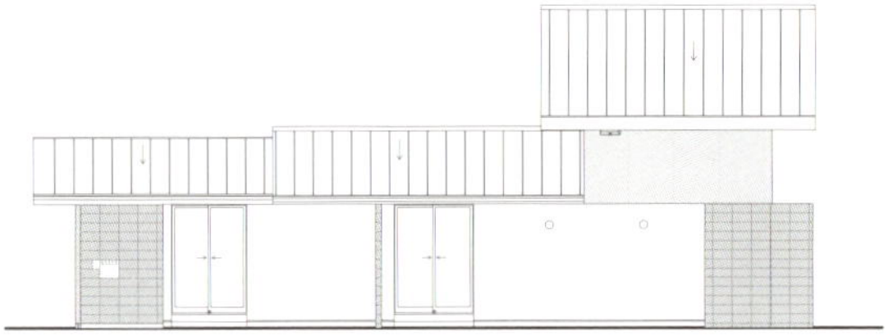

North elevation

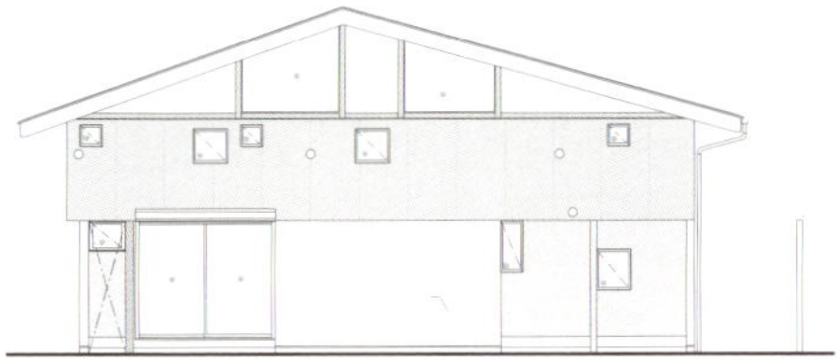

West elevation

The House in Furuedai

Design
Masato Sekiya

Location
Suita

Completion
2015

Area
978.3 square feet (90.89 square meters)

Photography
Akira Kita

At the rear of the garage is a stairwell that connects to the upper floors and floods the area with light, creating a bright continuous space. On the first floor, the living, dining, and kitchen area as well as a guest room are arranged to surround a courtyard, which is completely blocked off from the outside, creating privacy. On the second floor are private rooms. In the living room, the chimney of the fireplace placed there goes straight through the second floor to the roof, acting as a dynamic feature of the space. For the interior, the designer used older material to create the image of a traditional Japanese house, and the wooden areas were painted black to create a sense of unity.

Family members can work together at a kitchen bench connected to the table. For the bathroom, washbowl counter, and the hearth at the center of the living room, the designer used wood from trees grown in the owner's hometown. The owner was particularly fond of this feature. The bathroom and the washbasin area are separated from the living area by transparent tempered glass. For this reason, the space feels unified and cozy. The top of the bathtub has a window so that light comes in from outside, and occupants can see the garden courtyard from the bathroom window.

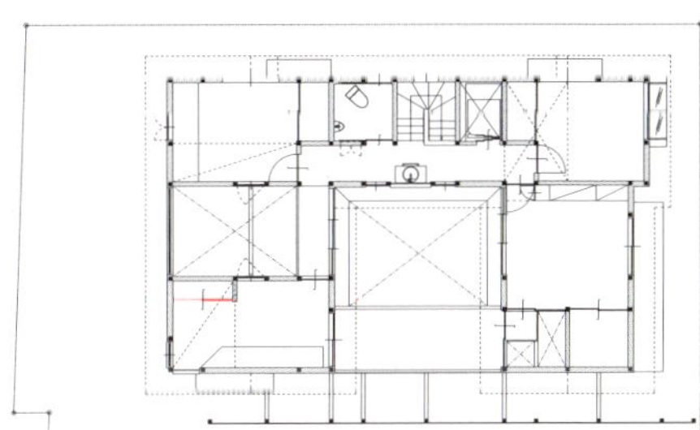

Third-floor plan

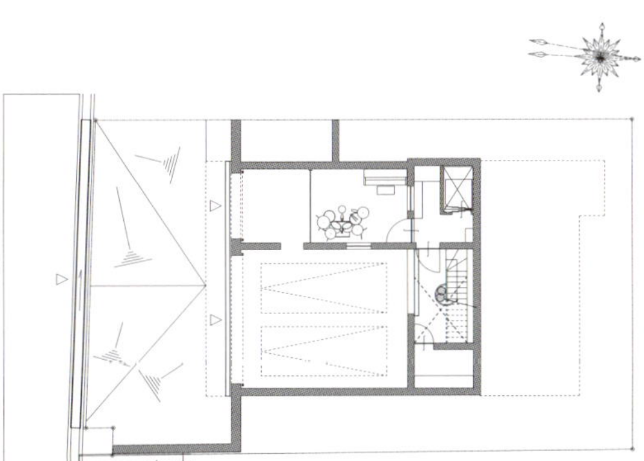

First-floor plan

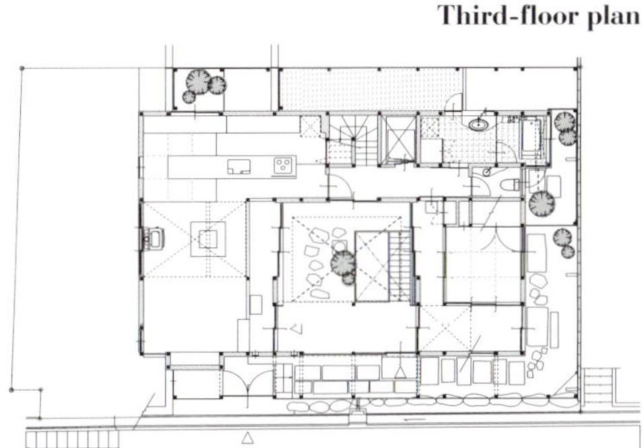

Second-floor plan

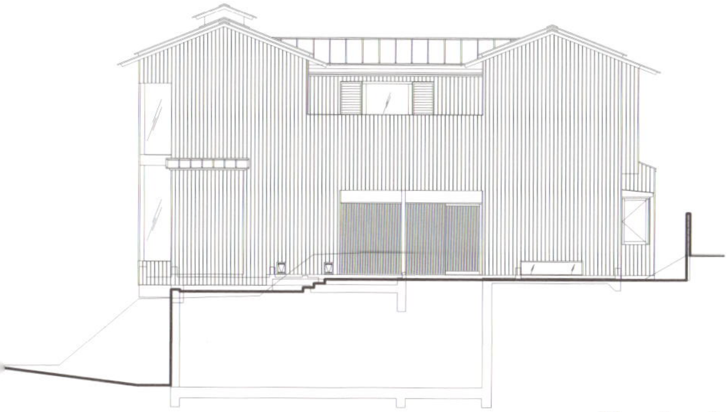

Elevation 1

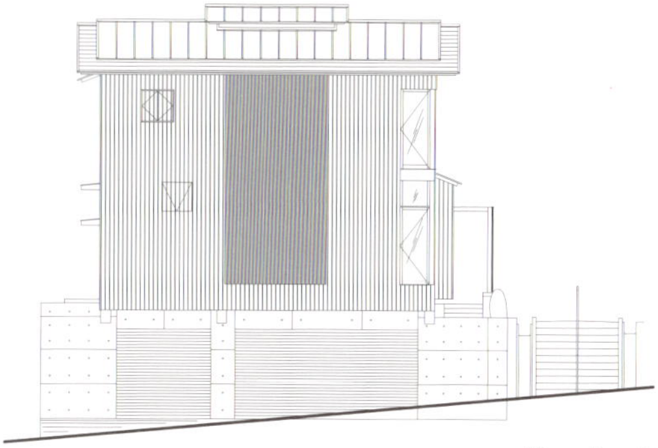

Elevation 2

The House in Yao

Design
Masato Sekiya

Location
Yao

Completion
2017

Area
1922.6 square feet (178.62 square meters)

Photography
Akira Kita

This project was the renovation of the main part of an old, traditional-style house. The site is rather narrow and extends from north to south, with narrow roads at each end bounding the property.

The designer renovated the main house to open up the courtyard and extended a deck about 9.8-foot-wide (3-meter-wide) across the courtyard to the single-floor building. The deck continues through the single-floor building, dividing it into east and west areas, and then continues to south. As a result, the view continues from the entrance of the main house on the north side to the garden in the south. In this way, the design takes advantage of the narrow shape of the site, connecting previously separated spaces.

The living and dining room area and the couple's bedroom can be bridged with sliding glass doors that can be opened completely, allowing the residents to selectively change the relationship between the deck and the living area. The old and new buildings are also connected with corridors that wrap around the building. The design enables the central courtyard garden to be in sight of people moving around inside the buildings so that they can enjoy the nature outside over the course of the year.

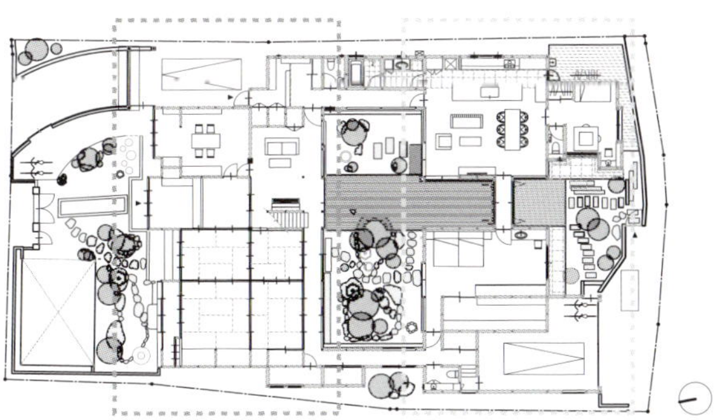

First-floor plan

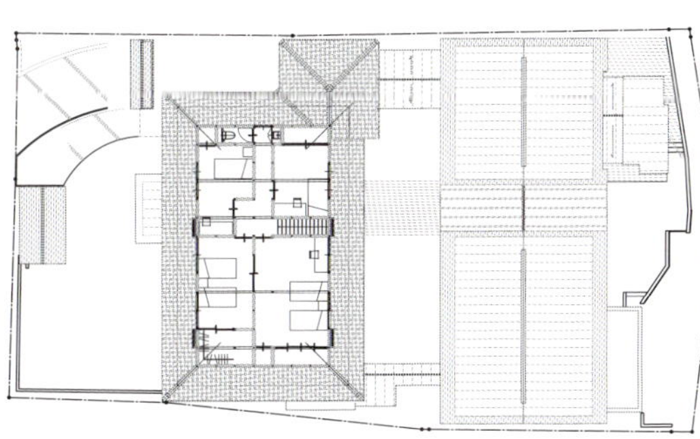

Second-floor plan

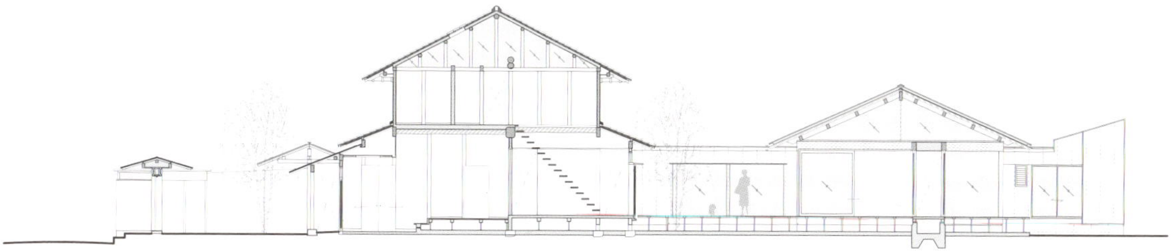

Section 1

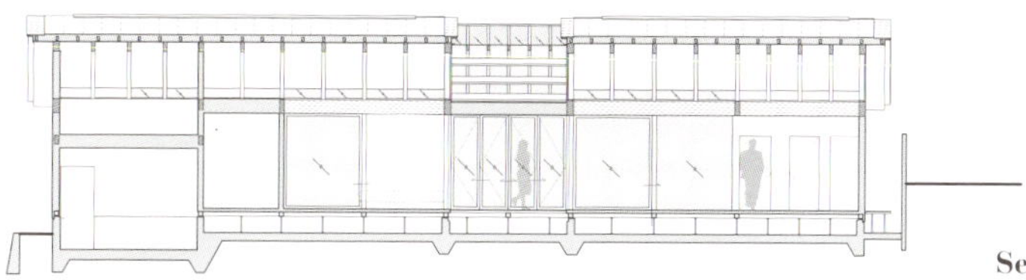

Section 2

Three of Roof House

Design
Takanobu Kishimoto

Location
Himeji

Completion
2014

Area
1147.5 square feet (106.61 square meters)

Photography
Eiji Tomita

By gradually lowering the height of the building from west to east, the sight line from the east neighbor was blocked, and the house gets the morning sun in each room as well as sunlight from the south between each space. The building holds a hobby room, a living room, as well as a walk-in-closet and plumbing area.

The common spaces, such as entrance, the study space for the children, and the dining area were placed in the center, between the above three rooms. By incorporating outside areas, such as parking and deck areas into the interior, a connection with the outside was created to make each individual space feel bigger.

This house, which is surrounded by three roofs, is bright and open while also allowing the whole family to enjoy the space both together and separately.

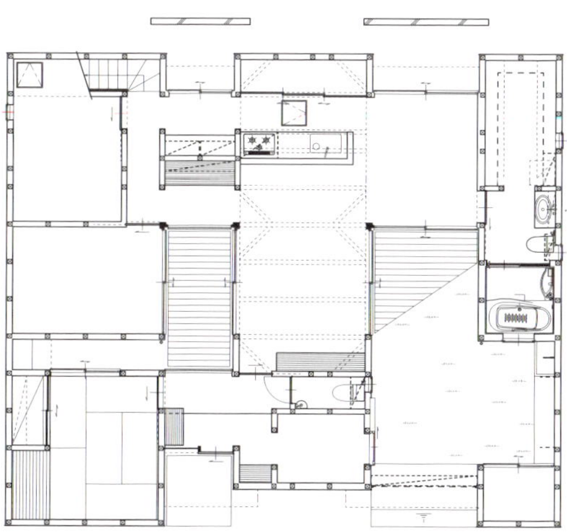

First-floor plan

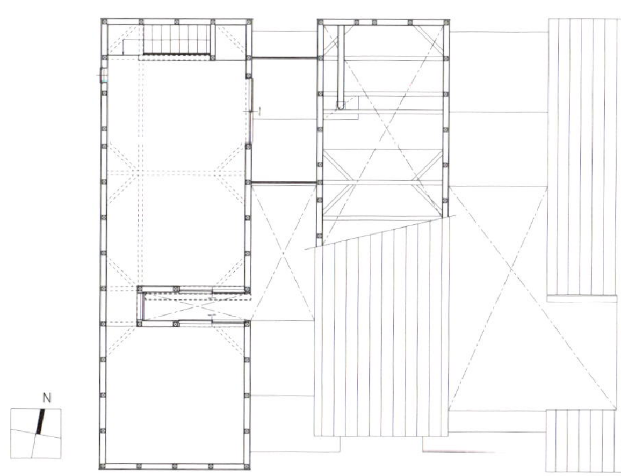

Second-floor plan

South elevation

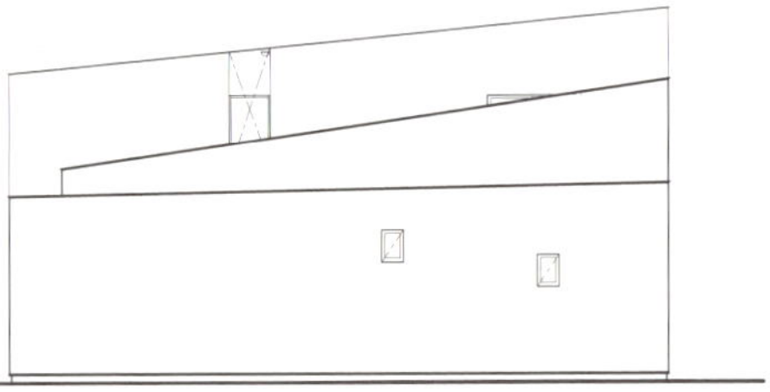

East elevation

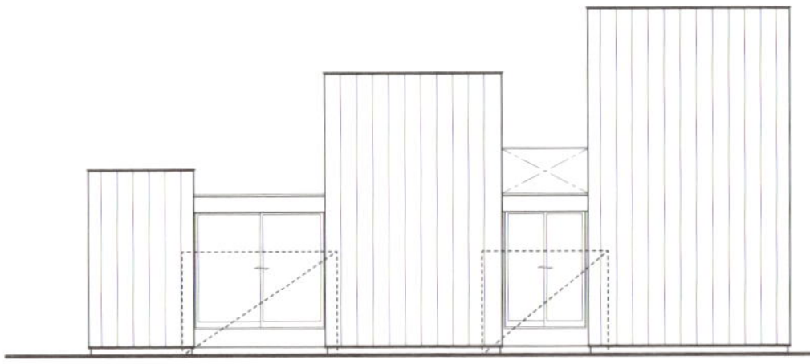

North elevation

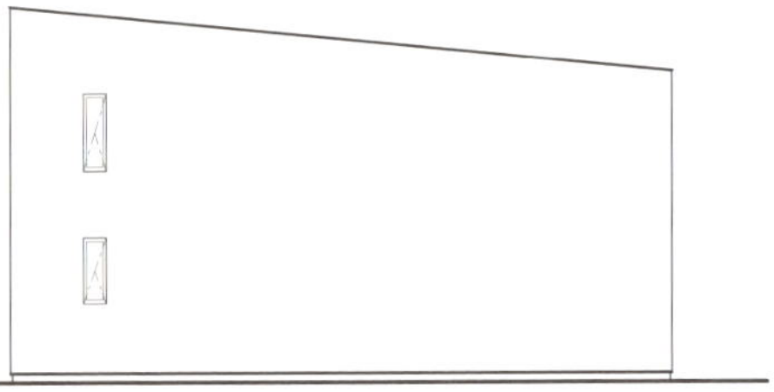

West elevation

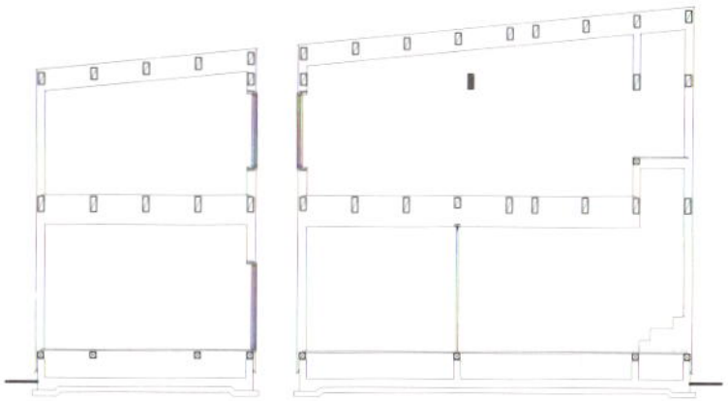

Section 1

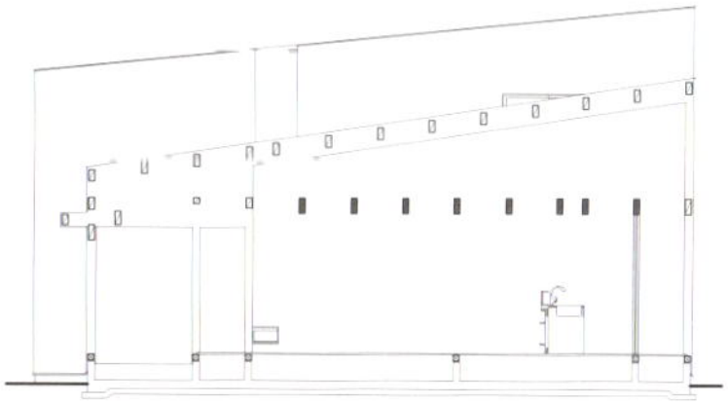

Section 2

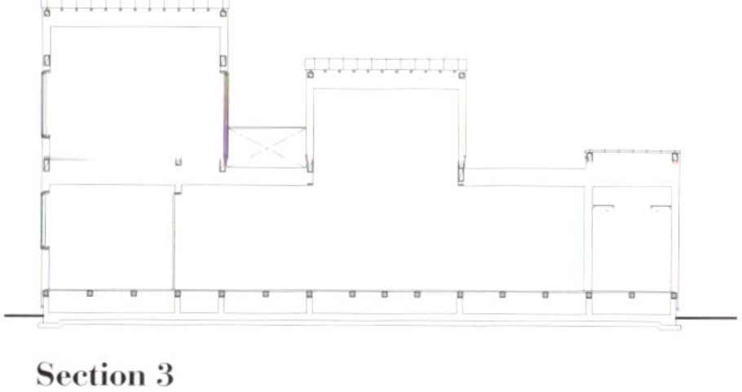

Section 3

Trays

Design
Akio Nakasa (Principal Architect),
Teppei Amano

Location
Sagamihara

Completion
2015

Area
2318.7 square feet (215.41 square meters)

Photography
Toshiyuki Yano

Trays utilizes the absolute maximum space construction regulations allowed on the lot. The porch, sandwiched between the walls with an arch opening, is a space in front of the door where the residents can put their bikes, while also serving as corridor to extend Trays.

The interior of Trays is finished in white, partitioned by grey walls to segment the porch, rooms, and balcony. All the rooms have lofts and a high ceiling, making the maximum height of the two-story apartment almost 32.8 feet (10 meters). In proportion to the height of the apartment, the outer walls of Trays are also high to ensure privacy from the outside, while the diagonally cut walls for the balcony and porch allow the influx of light and wind, defining the unique form of the building.

The state of the property where the house was built allowed for a three-story reinforced concrete apartment building. However, a two-story wooden apartment was chosen in consideration of rent. Being categorized according to building regulations as two-story wooden apartment with a loft, this apartment was designed as a quasi-maisonette with good loft space access.

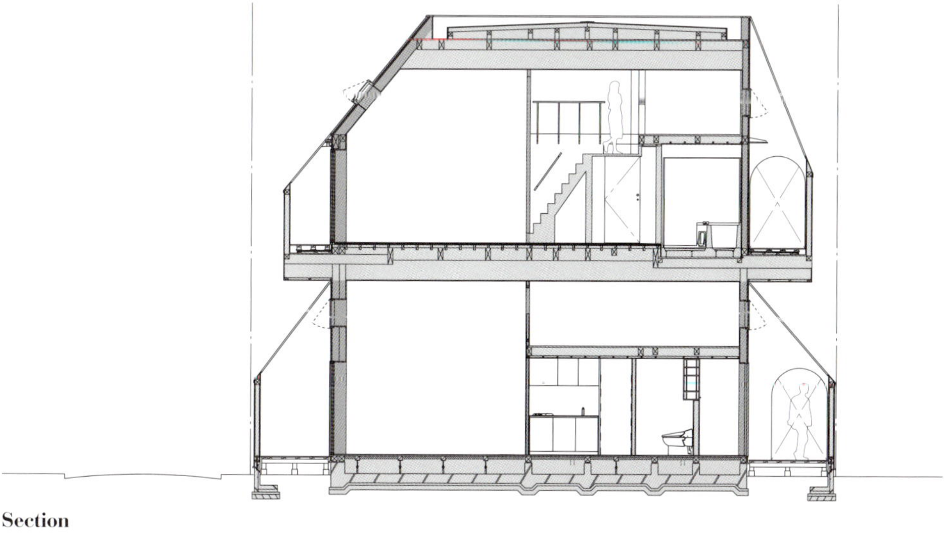

Section

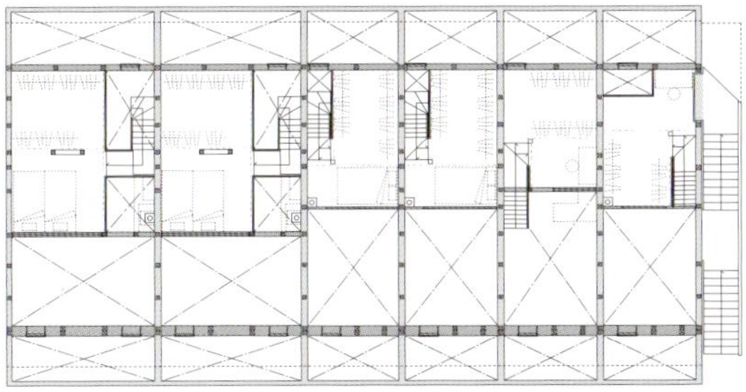

First-floor loft plan

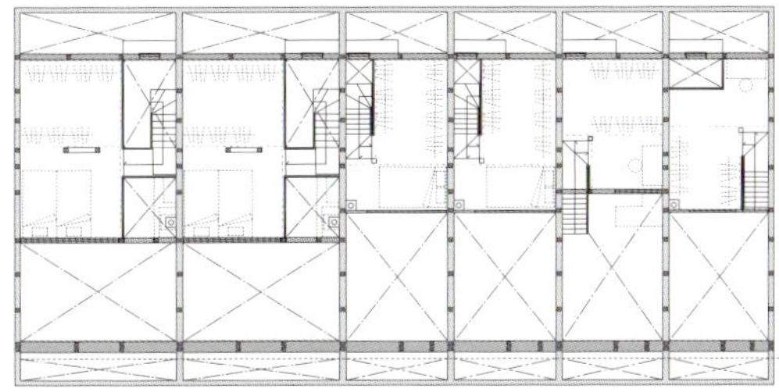

Second-floor loft plan

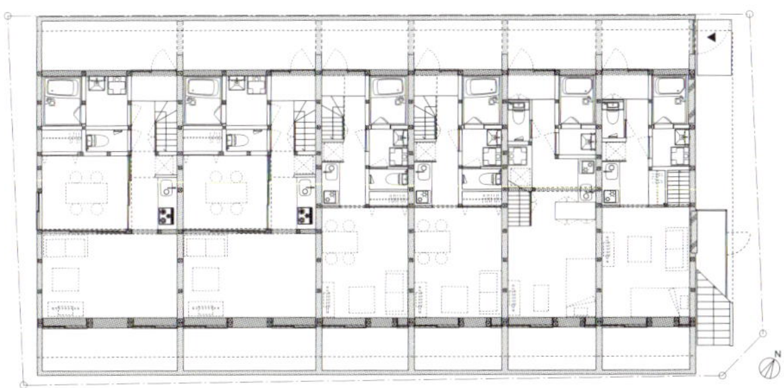

First-floor plan

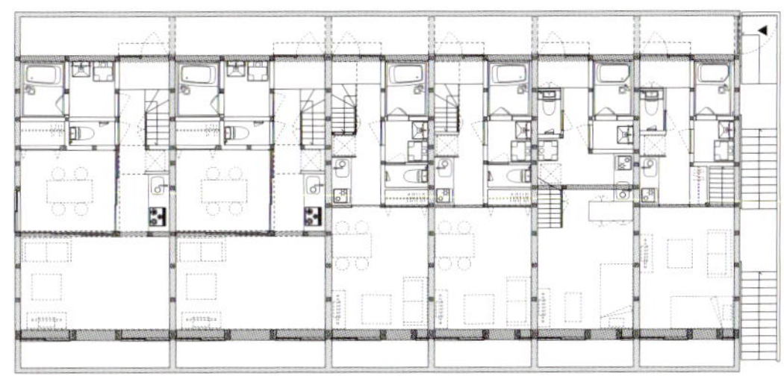

Second-floor plan

Wave

Design
Satoshi Kurosaki
(APOLLO Architects & Associates)

Location
Fujisawa

Completion
2014

Area
562.0 square feet (52.22 square meters)

Photography
Masao Nishikawa

The house has a U-shaped plan built around a courtyard on the ground floor. The courtyard is accessible directly from the outside, with a bathroom adjacent, allowing one to easily wash up after a day of surfing. The children's room, which is connected to the study, is also situated next to the courtyard so that they can comfortably study while enjoying the view of the family's memorial tree and the natural surroundings at the same time.

The second floor is an open space where everyone can look at the memorial tree in the courtyard below. The kitchen in the back is a convenient open-counter style and is connected to the dining room with a wide corner window. The living room is situated on the other side of the courtyard at the slightly lower level, connected to the dining room with a gently inclined ramp. The large roof balcony is situated on the street side, providing a sense of openness and protecting privacy at the same time. The window can be fully opened, connecting the interior and exterior spaces seamlessly.

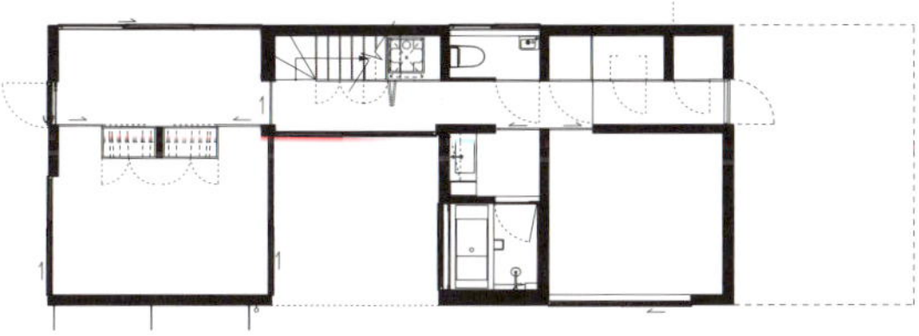

First-floor plan

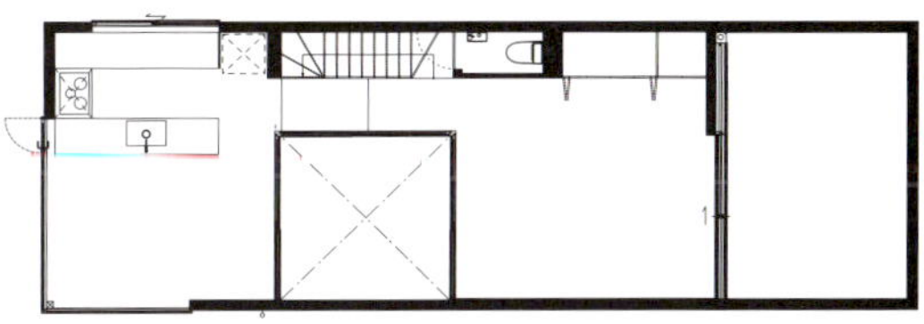

Second-floor plan

Where the Dune Used to Be

Design
Kazuhiko Kishimoto

Location
Fujisawa

Completion
2015

Area
1313.2 square feet (122 square meters)

Photography
Hiroshi Ueda

This place was originally a cluster of dunes surrounded by scattered pine trees, with gently sloping hills. The client requested the house design make efficient use of the hills. Therefore, the architect made a large stairway to the basement and a big bookshelf. Where to place the windows to enjoy the view had to be carefully reviewed, as the original pines still existed at the time of the housing development. That is why this symbolic large window of the house is open both to east and north, so the view will not get interrupted by any change that could result from development in the future. Consequently, they can enjoy both the rising and setting sun in the whole living area. The especially wonderful view of Mt. Fuji is available through the edge of the opening section on the west side.

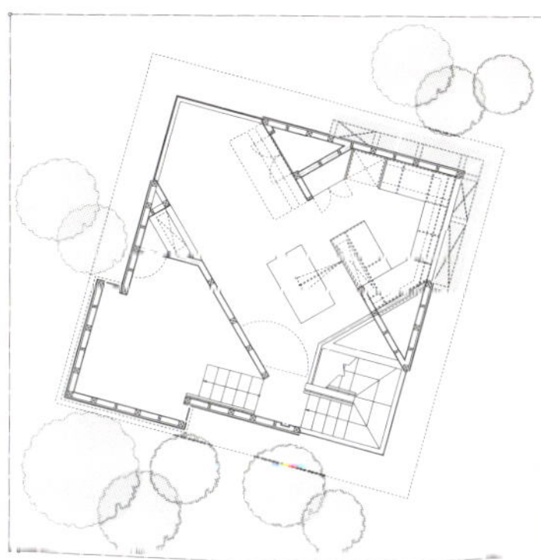

Second-floor plan

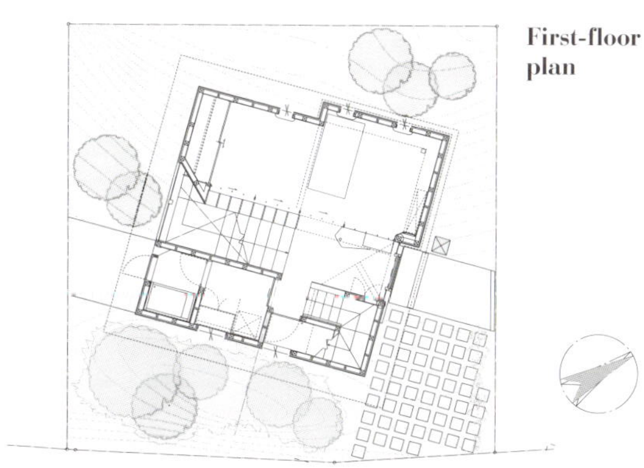

First-floor plan

Y8-house

Design
Masahiko Sato

Location
Nagasaki

Completion
2015

Area
1096 square feet (101.82 square meters)

Photography
Ikuma Satoshi

This house made of stone and wood was built in a residential area at the top of the hill in Sasebo, Nagasaki. The living area, dining area, office and a Japanese-style room on the second floor could be transformed into an open space with tatami mats when the movable screen for the Japanese-style room is removed. In addition, the ceiling lights in the living and dining rooms were designed to continuously move from the red cedar floor through the stone wall up to the ceiling, creating a rhythmic sense within a modern style.

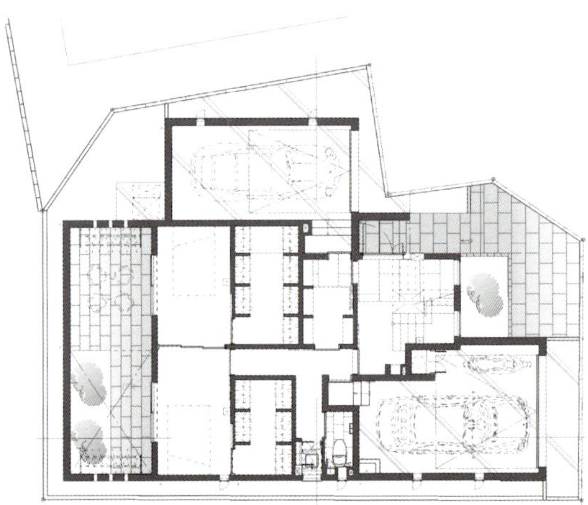

First-floor plan

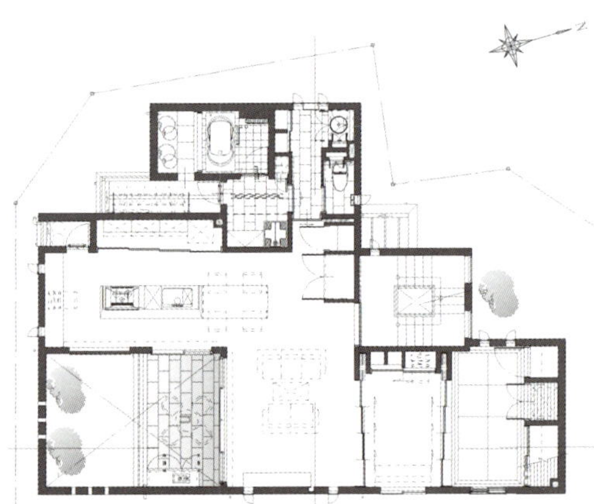

Second-floor plan

Y9-house

Design
Masahiko Sato

Location
Fukuoka

Completion
2016

Area
2405.2 square feet (223.45 square meters)

Photography
Koji Okamoto

In addition to protecting the privacy of the residents and mitigating crime, the main point of the proposed concept was how to capture and bring in the garden scenery on the east side into the living space inside the house.

The floor configuration of the building was designed so that the first floor not only became a parking area for existing clinic located on the adjacent property, but also an entrance to the elevator, a built-in garage space for the owners, and a staircase. On the second floor is a bedroom and guestroom, while on the third floor is a living and dining space where the family can gather together.

The ceiling on the parking space is outfitted with indirect lighting designed with polka dots of different diameter, adding festiveness to the space. The hallway leading to the elevator is partitioned from the parking space by a colonnade of red cedar wood on top of a half-height wall and vegetation.

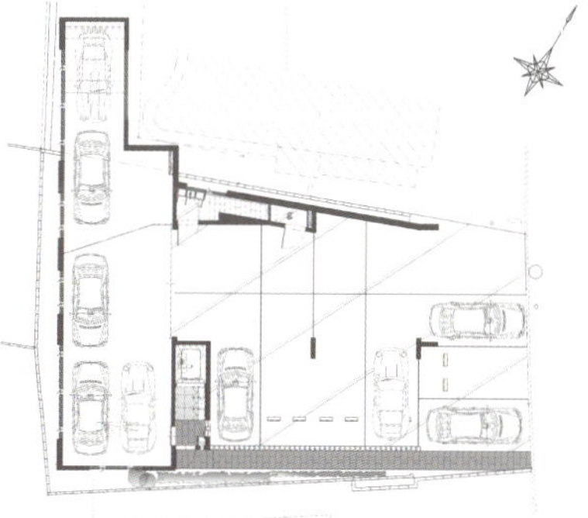

First-floor plan

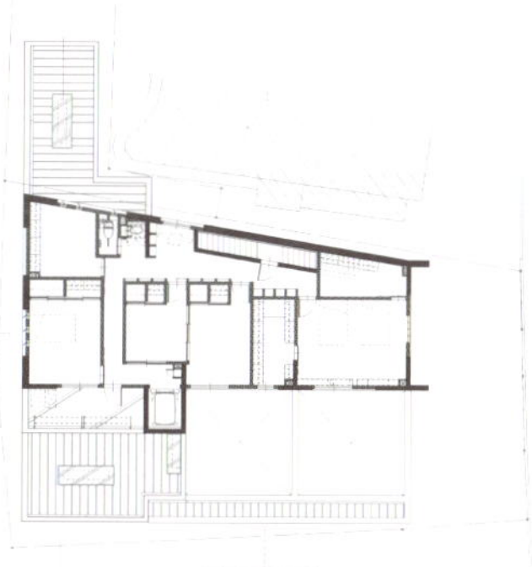

Second-floor plan

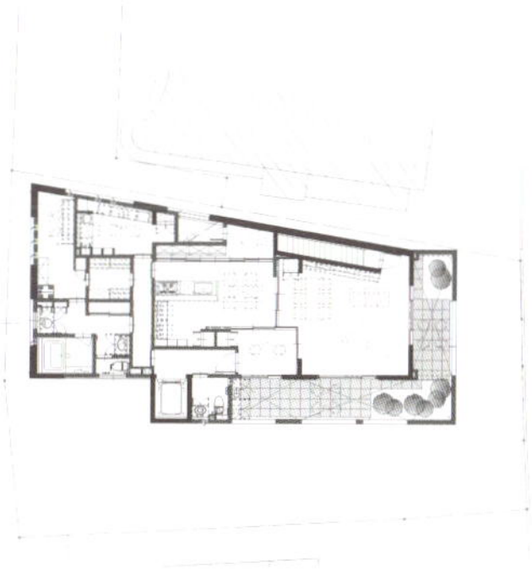

Third-floor plan

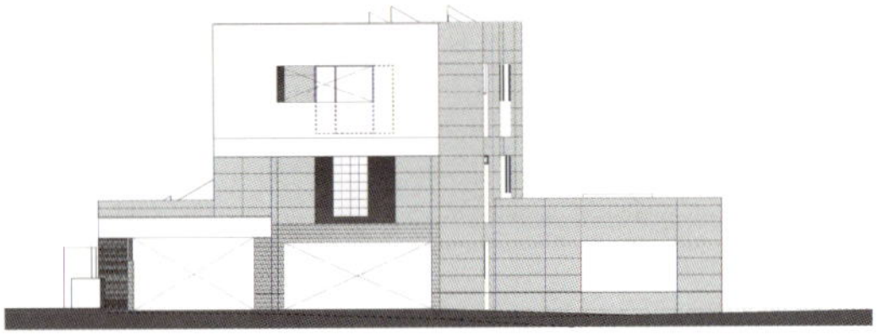

East elevation

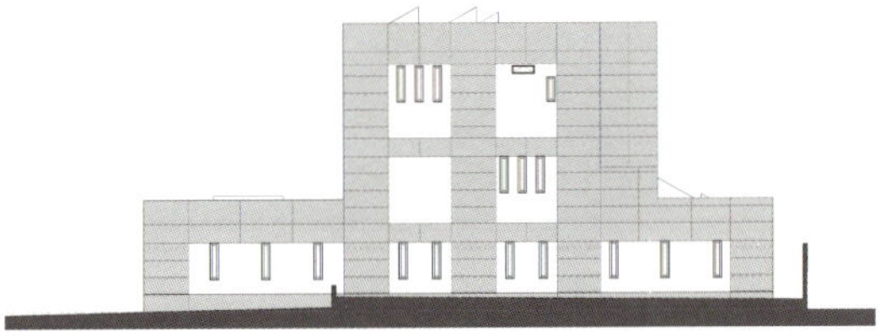

West elevation

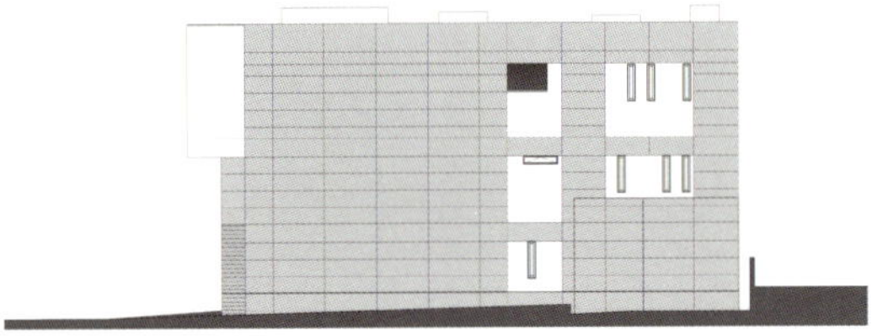

North elevation

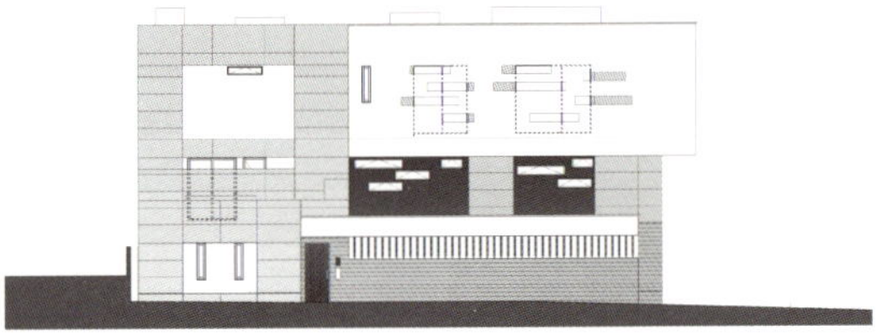

South elevation

Yamanote

Design
Katsutoshi Sasaki + Associates

Location
Toyota, Aichin

Completion
2014

Area
883.6 square feet (82.09 square meters)

Photography
Katsutoshi Sasaki + Associates

The architect designed a long dirt floor and located a bedroom, a kitchen, and a bathroom on the south side parallel to the dirt floor for ease of carrying out daily functions, such as eating, showering, and sleeping. The dirt floor is located on the lower end of the area that receives natural light.

The private rooms frame views of the outside, and facilitates the flow of light and heat throughout the building. The private rooms have a constant effect on the whole house because of their ability to bring in light and fresh air. The louver functions as partition between family areas because it partially blocks visibility.

Natural light passing through the windows is transformed by reflection, diffusion, and diffraction. The dynamic between the incoming natural light and the interior walls creates rich internal scenery.

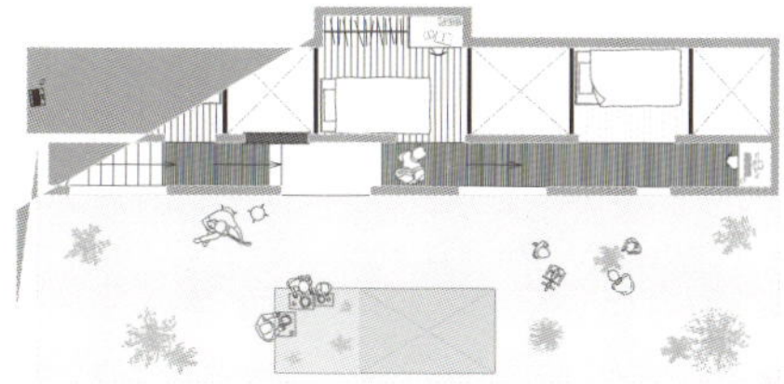

Second-floor plan

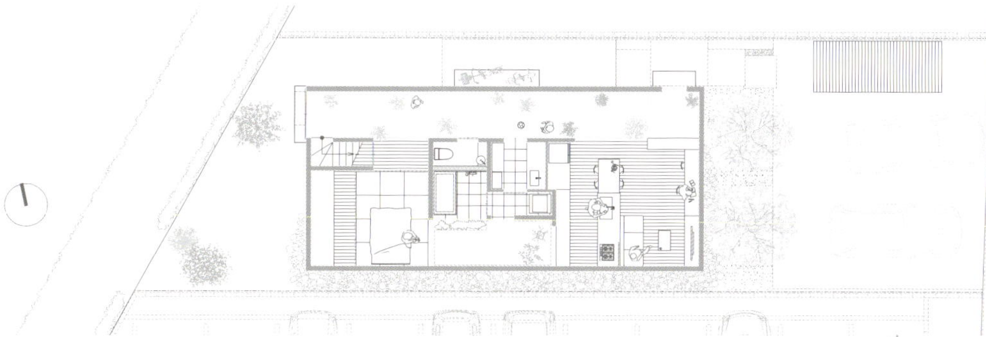

First-floor plan

Index

Kazuya Saito Architects
P 116

Website / kyst.jp
Address / 4-28 SUUT #403, Kasugamachi, Aoba-ku, Sendai, Miyagi 980-0821, Japan
Telephone / (+81) 22-221-0655

Kinoshita, Masahiro
PP 130, 190

Website / www.masahirokinoshita.com
Address / A101, 2-16-2 Shimoochiai, Shinjyuku-ku, Tokyo 161-0033, Japan
Telephone / (+81) 3-6908-3460

Kishimoto, Kazuhiko
PP 154, 102, 232

Website / www.ac-aa.com
Address / 4-15-40-403, Nakakaigan, Chigasaki, Kanagawa 253-0055, Japan
Telephone / (+81) 045-228-7072

Kishimoto, Takanobu
PP 8, 38, 98, 106, 124, 174, 222

Website / cd-aa.com
Address / 306 Oshima Building, 3-1-14, Kaigandori, Chuo-ku, Kobe, Japan
Telephone / (+81) 78-335-5795

Kochi Architect's Studio
P 12

Website / www.kkas.net
Address / Zoshigaya 2-17-1, Toshima-ku, Tokyo 171-0032, Japan
Telephone / (+81) 03-3986-0095

Komada Architects Office
P 138

Website / komada-archi.info
Address / #203/401, Nishikasai Apartments, Nishikasai 7-29-10, Edogawa-ku, Tokyo 134-0088, Japan
Telephone / (+81) 03-5679-1045

Muto, Keitaro
PP 46, 206

Website / mut-archi.com
Address / Imakomachi 29, Gifu, Gifu Prefecture 500-8069, Japan
Telephone / (+81) 058-215-7272

Naoi Architecture & Design Office
P 120

Website / www.naoi-a.com
Address / 2F-A, Kanda-Surugadai 3-1-9, Chiyoda-ku, Tokyo 101-0062, Japan
Telephone / (+81) 03-6273-7967

Principal Architect
P 226

Website / www.naf-aad.com
Address / Chatelet Sanyo 203, 8-12 Nishihirizuka cho, Naka-ku Hiroshima-shi, 730-0024, Japan
Telephone / (+81) 082-543-4602

Ryuichi Ashizawa Architects & associates
P 58

Website / www.r-a-architects.com
Address / 3F, Nakajima-BLD, 1-1-4 Nakazaki-nishi, Kita-ku, Osaka 530-0015, Japan
Telephone / (+81) 6-6485-2017

Sano, Fumihiko

P 150

Website / fumihikosano.jp
Address / 1F, Sasaki bld-B, 2-5-7,Koishikawa, Bunkyo-ku,Tokyo, 112-0002, Japan
Telephone / (+81) 050-3479-7320

Sato, Masahiko

PP 142, 234, 236

Website / www.architect-show.com
Address / 302 Royal Parks, Daimyo 8-18, 1 chome Daimyo, Chuo-ku, Fukuoka, Japan
Telephone / (+81) 092-762-2100

Sekiya, Masato

PP 102, 214, 218

Website / planet-creations.jp
Address / 33-1 Yoshida-Kaguraoka Town, Sakyo-ku, Kyoto City, Kyoto Prefecture 606-8311, Japan
Telephone / (+81) 075-200-6049

Shigeru Ban Architects

P 194

Website / www.shigerubanarchitects.com
Address / 5-2-4 Matsubara, Setagaya-ku, Tokyo, Japan
Telephone / (+81) (0)3-3324-6760

Shinichi Ogawa & Associates

PP 54, 128, 146

Website / shinichiogawa.com
Address / Central Park Tower 2911, 6-15-1 Nishi Shinjuku, Shinjuku-ku, Tokyo 160-0023, Japan
Telephone / (+81) 03-5323-2011

Shogo Aratani Architect & Associates

P 90

Website / www.ararchitect.com
Address / 2F, 3-10, Hazetsuka-cho, Nishinomiya, Hyogo, Japan
Telephone / (+81) 0798-31-3484

Shoji, Takeru

PP 32, 66

Website / www.takerushoji.jp
Address / #202, Ijinike house, 591-1 Nishiohatacho, Chuo-ku, Niigata 951-8104, Japan
Telephone / (+81) 25-227-6639

SNARK

PP 82, 148

Website / snark.cc
Address / 53-2, Tamachi, Takasaki-shi, Gunma Prefecture, 370-0824, Japan
Telephone / (+81) 027-384-2268

Spatial Design Studio

P 186

Website / www.s-d-s.net
Address / #37, Yaraicho Terrace 101, Yaraichomachi, Shinjuku-ku, Tokyo 162-0805, Japan
Telephone / (+81) 03-3266-9971

Suga, Shotaro

PP 74, 78

Website / sugaatelier.com
Address / 1-3-20, Bandai , Abeno-ku, Osaka 545-0036, Japan
Telephone / (+81) 6-6626-1920

studio LOOP
PP 134, 178

Website / www.studioloop.net
Address / 3-8-4 Asahino, Itakura, Oura, Gunma Prefecture 374-0112, Japan
Telephone / (+81) 0276-82-5730

Takagi, Yoshichika
P 104

Website / yoshichikatakagi.com
Address / 11-5-9, Shinkotoni9jo, Kita-ku, Sapporo, Hokkaido 001-0909, Japan
Telephone / (+81) 011-769-9071

Tenkyu, Kazunori
P 6

Website / k-tenk.com
Address / 1-13-10 2nd floor, Marunouchi, Kita-ku, Okayama-shi, Okayama 700-0823, Japan
Telephone / (+81) 86-235-5516

Tsuchida, Takuya
PP 198, 202

Website / www.number555.com
Address / Bluff gatehouse 26, Yamate-cho, Naka-ku, Yokohama-shi, Kanagawa 231-0862, Japan
Telephone / (+81) 045-567-7179

Yahagi, Masao
P 16

Website / www.myahagi.com
Address / Tounoharu 5-10-8, Higashi-ku, Fukuoka City, Fukuoka 813-0001, Japan
Telephone / (+81) 092-719-0456

y+M design office
P 210

Website / ymdo.net
Address / 1F, Hayashi Towel Building, 3-3-7 Yasakadai, Suma-ku, Kobe, Hyogo Prefecture, 654-0161, Japan
Telephone / (+81) 78-891-7616

Published in Australia in 2018 by
The Images Publishing Group Pty Ltd
Shanghai Office
ABN 89 059 734 431
6 Bastow Place, Mulgrave, Victoria 3170, Australia
Tel: +61 3 9561 5544 Fax: +61 3 9561 4860
books@imagespublishing.com
www.imagespublishing.com

The Images Publishing Group Reference Number: 1500

NATIONAL LIBRARY OF AUSTRALIA

A catalogue record for this book is available from the National Library of Australia

Title: Japanese Residence
Author: Takahiro Ohashi [Ed.]
ISBN: 9781864708080

Printed by Everbest Printing Investment Limited, in Hong Kong/China